The Complete Keto Diet Guide for Beginners After 50:

28-Day Meal Plan for Fast & Easy Weight Loss | Cookbook with 110 Low-Carb Recipes for Seniors. Improve Your Health and Reset Your Metabolism.

AMY STEPHENS

TABLE OF CONTENTS

Introduction

The Ketogenic Diet follows a fairly simple principle: keep your food consumption low-carb and high-fat. So basically, being on the diet means eating less carbohydrates and adding more fats in your daily meals. Don't be confused. When we say "fat" we're not talking about the literal kind that's attached to your body. Fat has gotten a bad reputation nowadays, but "fat" the nutrient is very different from the "fat" that makes your clothes fit tight.

Good fats are the kind you get from avocado, nuts, and fish. For example, omega-3 and omega-6 fatty acids can help you lose weight, get better heart health, and have excellent hair and nails.

What Happens to Your Body When You Eat Keto?

Before talking about how to do Keto – it's essential to consider why this particular diet works. What happens to your body that makes you lose weight?

As you probably know, the body uses food as its fuel. Everything you eat is turned into energy, so that you can get up and do whatever you need to accomplish for the day. So how does it work? Our primary source of energy is sugar. So, when you eat, your body breaks down the food's molecules into glucose, then this sugar is processed into energy. If you eat just the right amount of food, then your body is fueled for the whole day. If you overeat, then the sugar is stored in your body – hence the accumulation of fat.

But what happens if you eat less food? This is where the Ketogenic Diet comes in. You see, the process of creating sugar from food is usually faster if the food happens to be rich in carbohydrates. Bread, rice, grain, pasta – all of these are carbohydrates, and they are the easiest food types to turn into energy.

So, the Ketogenic Diet is all about reducing the amount of carbohydrates you eat. Does this mean you won't get the kind of energy you need for the day? Of course not! It only means that now, your body must find other possible sources of energy. Do you know where it will get that from? Your stored body fat!

Here's the way it works – you are eating less carbohydrates every day. The body breaks down the stored fat and turns it into molecules called ketone bodies, which replace glucose in keeping you energetic. This process is called "ketosis" and obviously, this is where the name of the Ketogenic Diet comes from. As long as you keep your carbohydrates reduced, the body will keep getting its energy from your body fat.

Sounds Simple, Right?

The Ketogenic Diet is often praised for its simplicity, and when you look at it correctly, the process is straightforward. The science behind the diet's effectivity is also well-documented and has been proven multiple times by different medical fields. For example, an article on Diet Review by Harvard provided a lengthy discussion on how the Ketogenic Diet works and why it is so useful for those who choose to use it.

But Fat Is the Enemy...Or Is It?

No – fat is NOT the enemy. Unfortunately, years of bad science told us that fat is something you have to avoid. But it's actually a beneficial thing for weight loss! Before we move forward with this book, we'll have to discuss exactly what "healthy fats" are and why they're the good guys. In order to do this, we need to make a distinction between the different kinds of fat. You have probably heard of them before, but it can still be a bit confusing. We will try to go through them as simply as possible:

Saturated fat. Saturated fat is something you can find in meat, dairy products, and other processed food items. It's also called "solid fat" because each molecule is packed with hydrogen atoms. For years, they have been considered as "bad fats" because of the increase in cholesterol levels that they bring. But our body actually needs that molecule! And it only becomes the "bad guy" when the body is in an inflammatory state, due to an excess of sugar, for example. Later in the recipes, you'll find that the Ketogenic Diet promotes both saturated and unsaturated fats, since many studies implied that there is no proven correlation between the assumption of saturated fats and various diseases that were considered.

Unsaturated Fat. These are the ones dubbed as healthy fat. They're the kind of fat you find in avocado, nuts, and other ingredients used in Keto-friendly recipes. They're known to lower blood cholesterol and come in two types: polyunsaturated and monounsaturated. Both are good for your body, but the benefits slightly vary, depending on what you're consuming.

Polyunsaturated fat. These are perhaps the best in the list. You can get them mostly from vegetable and seed oils such as olive oil, coconut oil, and more. They are also found in deep sea fish like tuna, herring, and salmon. You know about omega-3 fatty acids, right? They're often suggested against heart diseases, since they can lower their risks by as much as 19 percent (according to Pub Med's study: "Effects on coronary heart diseases of increased poly-unsaturated fat in lieu of saturated fat: systematic review & meta-analysis of randomized controlled tests").

Chapter 1: What Is Ketogenic Diet

In very blunt terms, the Keto diet is a low-carb diet that aims to shift the way your body processes food. Typically, your body thrives on the carbohydrates you give it, and it uses those carbohydrates to boost your blood sugar. The only problem with that boost is that *what goes up, must come down!*

Have you ever been sitting at your desk past two in the afternoon and it suddenly feels like your head is a cinder block? Blood sugar crashes can take all the wind out of your sails and they're far more likely to occur when you're allowing your body to get all of its energy from carbohydrates.

When you start Keto, you are cutting your carbohydrates down to only 5% of your daily macronutrient intake, with a limit of 20 grams per day. It's essential to track what you're taking into your body for the first few weeks in order to do it correctly.

This diet works by balancing your food intake between a majority of fats and a particular amount of protein. By giving your body very calculated measurements of all the macros, your body is forced to run not only on the fat you're giving it but also on the fat that your body has stored over the years. In fact, so many of us have stores of stubborn fat that simply won't leave us.

The answer is to give your body no choice but to burn that fat to keep going!

What are its Advantages?

By diminishing the carbohydrates intake, you are giving your body an *alternative fuel source*. It shifts over to a different metabolism mode that activates a constant state of fat burning.

With the stored fat that so many of us are trying to get rid of, the body has a fuel source to run on *always*. This can lead to so much more energy than you had before, so get ready to feel the urge to get out and play!

You will find that fat loss comes to you with far less effort than you realized was possible. Because that fat-burning machine within you is working around the clock, the fat will disappear before too long.

As we come up over the age of 50, so many of us have resigned ourselves to having that bit of excess fat that has never gone away, no matter what exercise, no matter what diet, no matter *what*. With Keto, those problem areas are no longer the exception to the rule. When your body burns fat, it burns all of it!

Many who have tried this diet have seen that it makes drastic changes to their quality of life, health, the clarity of their skin, and even the resolution and improvement of severe physical disorders like type II diabetes!

One of the most popular aspects of it, is that you don't have to sacrifice flavor and the foods that taste the best to obtain the best results. There are cheesy, creamy, delicious dishes as well as bright, fresh, and crisp ones. Keto is all about achieving a perfect balance, keeping that balance, and allowing your body to thrive on what it has.

Things to Keep in Mind

One of the biggest misconceptions when it comes to Keto is that all fat is created equal, which simply isn't true. You want to consider the types of fats you're eating so you're giving your body what it needs to thrive, repair, and keep going.

While things like beef, bacon, pork chops, and cheese are perfectly okay to have on Keto, it's a great idea to make sure that you're also getting plenty of unsaturated fats, nutrient-rich roughage, and healthy proteins alongside that. Having bacon and eggs for breakfast is allowed, and a salad for lunch is a great follow-up.

One must also remember that *Keto is not a high-protein diet*. It's a low-carb, high-fat diet that relies on a specific balance between fat, protein, and carbohydrates to give your body the best fat burning possible. Your body does need protein, but an excessive amount could set you back in your weight loss progress, so keep your eyes keen for that.

While this is not a calorie-counting diet, this doesn't mean that there is no limit to the amount that you can eat. In fact, if you can ballpark your intake to 2,000 calories per day or fewer, you will see much more effective results than you would if you were to surpass that on a consistent basis.

Also, with this diet, your body tends to purge a large amount of your stored electrolytes. It's important to drink plenty of water throughout the day (yes, I'm sorry, you're going to be peeing *all the time*), and you will have to find a supplemental source of electrolytes to add to your daily intake. This will keep you from feeling run-down, tired, or dehydrated while you're doing Keto!

Chapter 2: Why Is It Important For People Over 50?

Now comes the interesting part. I am sure you have been wondering how it will help you, a person who is 50 years or more in age, and why is it so important, right? Do not worry as I shall provide you with an answer that satisfies both questions.

A few minutes ago, we read how Keto diet pushes our body into ketosis- a state where ketones take over the role of glucose. That may sound good for younger people than you, but the fact is that it is actually a better fit for someone your age. Why, I hear you ask?

As you grow in age, the body's natural fat burning ability reduces. When that happens, your body stops receiving a healthy dose of nutrients properly, which is why you could be more likely to develop diseases and ailments. With the Keto diet, you are pushing the body into ketosis and bypassing the need to worry about your body's ability to burn fat. Once in ketosis, your body will now burn fat forcefully for its survival.

Once more, your system will now start to regain strength. An even better aspect that follows is the drop in your insulin level. If you are someone diagnosed with diseases such as type 2 diabetes and others, this might even weaken the symptoms or eliminate the diseases from your body altogether.

There are studies underway, and most of them suggest that Keto is far more beneficial to those above 50 than it is for those under this age bracket. A quick search on Google and you are immediately overwhelmed with over 93 million results, most of which explain the benefits of this diet for people above 50. That is a staggering number for a diet plan that has only been around for a few years.

It is also important to highlight that as we get older, we start losing more than just the ability to burn fat. During this phase of our lives, we come across various obstacles. Some of them are natural, they transpire because our body is no longer able to function at the same rate as before. Ketogenic diet helps us regain that edge and feel energized from within.

There are hundreds of thousands of stories, all pointing out how this revolutionary diet is especially helpful for older adults and the elderly. It is therefore a no-brainer for people above 50 who have spent ages trying to find the perfect diet for them. With such a high success rate, there is no harm in trying, right?

Before the Keto phenomenon, there was the Atkins diet. This was also a low carb diet, just like its Keto counterpart, and it also became a huge hit with the masses. However, unlike Keto, the Atkins diet provided weight loss while putting a person through constant hunger. Keto, on the other hand, takes away that element, and it does that using ketosis.

Constant exposure to ketosis reduces appetite, hence taking away the biggest hurdle in most diets. The Atkins diet failed to address that front, which is why it was more of a hit and miss. However, credit where it is due, the Atkins diet did garner quite a bit of fame. But, since the inception of Keto, things have changed dramatically.

A study was conducted where 34 overweight adults were monitored and observed for 12 months. All of them were put on Keto diets. The result showed that participants had lower HbA1c (hemoglobin A1C) levels, experienced significant weight loss, and were more likely to discontinue their medications for diabetes completely.

All in all, the Keto diet is shaping up to be quite a promising candidate for older adults. Not only will this diet allow us to lead a healthier lifestyle, but it will also curb our ailments and ensure high energy around the clock. That is quite the resume for a diet, and one that now seems too attractive to pass up. This is the point where I made up my mind and decided to give the Keto diet a go, and I recommend the same to you.

Whether you are a man or a woman, if you have put on weight, or you are suffering from ailments like type 2 diabetes, consider this as your ticket to a care-free world where you will lead a healthy life and rise out of the ailments eventually.

Keto has been producing results which have attracted the top minds and researchers for a fairly long time. Considering the unique nature of this lifestyle of eating, the results have been rather encouraging.

"Great! How do I start?"

Not so fast. While the Keto diet is simple, there are a few things I should point out. Some of these might even change your mind about the entire diet plan, but if you are determined for a healthy lifestyle and a fit body, I assure you these should not be of much trouble.

Preparing Yourself for Keto

When entering the world of Keto, quite a few of us just pick up a recipe on the internet and start cooking things accordingly. While that is good, we can often be found asking ourselves these questions: what would happen if I replace nuts with something else? Is oatmeal a part of Keto diet? What are Keto approved food items? Are there any risks involved?

Here is some more information regarding such questions:

• Keto is an extremely strict food diet where you can only eat things which can be classified as Keto worthy. Anything that falls out of this category is a straight "no!"

• Keto is a completely new lifestyle. That means your body will undergo some changes. While most of these will be good, some may pose problems such as the "Keto flu". Most of the people I know, including myself, faced this "flu" with similar symptoms to influenza. It was only after some research that I realized this was natural. The Keto flu is not exactly alarming, but it is best to be mentally prepared for it.

• You will need to work on your cooking skills as Keto strictly pushes processed, high carb foods out of the diet.

• If you aren't really into the idea of protein and fat intake, you may wish to reconsider this diet, as these are the two primary areas that Keto focuses on.

Apart from this, there are some mistakes people tend to make when they begin their journey. Some of the most common mistakes are:

• **Not knowing the Keto food properly:** Just because something looks like a Keto-friendly item, it doesn't mean it is Keto approved. Always refer to some food guide to check if the item you are interested in is a part of the "good food" in Keto.

• **Keeping the same level of fat intake throughout:** This often leads to results which show in the start and then disappear. You need to constantly adjust your diet and monitor your protein and fat intake.

• **Thinking the Keto flu is the only issue to face:** There are other difficulties which will emerge within the first 10 weeks of your Keto journey. This will include lethargic limbs, which will make walking difficult at first. Owing to the change in fiber intake, you may either face diarrhea or constipation as well.

• **Pushing bodies with vigorous exercises:** You have just started Keto, give your body a bit of time to adjust. Keep things slow and steady.

- **Not replenishing on electrolytes:** Since we mentioned exercise and possibly, diarrhea, your body will run low on electrolytes faster than usual. This is something that you may want to keep in check. Think sodium and potassium!

These are some of the most common mistakes people have made, and surprisingly, even *I* was no exception! If only I had someone to properly guide me, back then.

So now, you know the "what" and the "how" of Keto, but you are yet to figure out whether this diet is meant for women or men. As a part of the first step, I will now provide you with more details regarding both sides and you will also be given a breakdown of facts to see just how beneficial this diet is for anyone.

Chapter 3: How To Get Started with the Ketogenic Diet When You're Over 50?

Jumping on the Keto wagon, as well as committing to anything, can be an intimidating attempt. However, getting started with this one is relatively simple. No matter how many forms of the Keto diet there are out there, they share some similarities:

Restrict Carbohydrates: This is the entire point of a Keto diet – little carbs intake. A Keto diet should have less than 20g of *net carbs* a day, although some people can go up to 30g. If you can get this right, then you are well on your way to become successful in your Ketogenic diet adventure. Other than that, there are a few more things to keep in mind:

1. **Limit protein intake**: A Keto diet consists mostly of fat, not carbs or protein. Too much protein can put undue stress on your kidneys. Also, the excess will be converted to glucose, then stored as fat anyway. So, make sure that you get your protein portion right as well. This should be the second priority, after setting your daily carbs limit.

2. **Use fat as a lever**: Fat isn't necessarily a bad thing - especially in a Keto diet - because fat makes up a huge portion of your regime. This is because fat is both a source of energy and satiety. Here, fat serves as a lever, whereas carbs and protein remain constant. That means you can determine how much weight you want to gain or lose based on how much fat you consume. Because our goal is to lose weight, that means you need to eat just enough fat. No more, no less.

3. **Drink water**: Water is especially important in a Keto diet. Your body usually needs it to store glycogen in the liver. When you eat foods low in carbs, the body uses up glycogen so you can burn fat, which means depleting your water store as well. That means you will become dehydrated faster. You normally need 2 gallons a day, but I recommend going up to 3 or 4 gallons a day when you are on a Keto diet.

4. **Take care of the electrolytes**: Since a Keto diet uses up water, that means losing electrolytes as well. Potassium, sodium, and magnesium are the major electrolytes in our body. When you do not have enough of them, you feel sick. This is commonly referred to as the "Keto flu". You do not have to endure it, as long as you keep your electrolytes at a sufficient level. That means salting your food, drinking bone broth or

any other broth, and eating pickled veggies. If any of these alternatives are unfavorable for you, you can also take supplements to top up your electrolytes store, but make sure to consult your doctor before doing that.

5. **Eat when you are hungry**: Some people have the mindset that they need to eat at least 4 to 6 meals, or even snack constantly between mealtimes. No wonder they gain weight. In a Keto diet, frequent eating is not recommended as it can interfere with your weight loss effort. So, only eat when you are hungry. If you don't feel hungry, then do not eat. Anyhow, this part should be easy, considering that a Keto diet - like any other low-carb diet - lacks in carbohydrates, so it naturally suppresses appetite altogether.

6. **Focus on whole foods**: You do not have to resort to eating only natural or whole food so you can get your carbs limit down properly. However, keep in mind that processed food is rich in carbs and will not help you get rid of cravings, not to mention that they are unhealthy in the first place.

7. **Exercise**: This is optional, but you should take care of your muscles at your age as they start to degrade. You will feel better, your health will improve, and your weight will go down faster.

Keto Macro

If you really want to get it down, you will need an online calculator to help you determine how much you need to eat. It is impossible to give you a direct formula because there are many variables to take into consideration. But if you are curious, a Keto diet usually contains the following:

- Fat: 60% to 75%
- Protein: 15% to 30%
- Net carbs: 5% to 10%

Fat, protein, and net carbs content vary from person to person, but they all stay within this range. It is worth mentioning that the sum of all three should equal 100%. The percentage is the amount of the daily calorie intake.

Chapter 4: What Are The Best Fats On Keto?

Fats are the most important part of the Keto diet, but which fats are best for the diet? As we mentioned before, there are a variety of fats that can be used. The fat eaten on the Keto diet makes up 70% of the food that you'll be eating each day. This makes the types of fats eaten important, because not all of them are going to result in a healthy weight loss. There are some of them that should be consumed more regularly, and others which consumption should be limited. Just because it's the predominant macro, it doesn't mean that its unlimited consumption is part of the Keto diet. Stay within your calorie allotment for the day and watch your macros. Do not exceed your macros when you're eating fats. Most importantly, consume the correct types of fat to maximize the effectiveness of your weight loss.

Types of Fat

There are several types of fat and some are better than others when it comes to overall health and usefulness as fuel for the body. Combine various types of fats that have proved to be the best fuel for the body.

Polyunsaturated Fatty Acids (PUFA)

This is the category where omega-3 fatty acids fall. Omega-3 fatty acids are good for the brain and should be included in a healthy diet. The problems with PUFAs arise when they are heated because they may, with heat, form compounds that cause inflammation and that could damage the pancreas and liver. So, it's best to consume them cold.

Some good PUFAs for the Keto diet are linseed and hemp oils, nuts, algae, chia seeds and fatty fish, such as salmon.

Monounsaturated Fatty Acids (MUFAs)

These fats are the healthiest of unsaturated fats. They remain stable when heated and have a positive effect on insulin production and cholesterol levels. MUFAs assist the pancreas in producing a consistent level of insulin. They are also known to improve overall blood pressure and heart health.

The MUFAs are commonly found in olive and sesame oil, avocadoes, macadamia nuts, butter, and lard. These oils can be moderately included in the Keto diet.

Saturated Fats

These are the best fats for Keto. They are found both in animal and vegetable sources. While following a Keto regime, hunger can be assuaged by the consumption of saturated fats. These fats have a positive influence on our health. Included in saturated fats is MCT oil. "MCT" stands for "Medium Chain Triglycerides". The shorter length of triglyceride makes MCTs easier to digest and break down in the system. MCTs are known to improve brain function and reduce the growth of yeast and bacteria in the body. It is a beneficial oil while on Keto.

There is also an improvement to the immune system and an increase in bone density when saturated fats are present in our diet. This is a good side effect for women over 50 who may be suffering from bone loss.

Common foods that are good sources of healthy saturated fats are coconut or palm oil, butter and ghee, eggs and fatty meats like steak or lard. These items should be included in the Keto diet for it is the healthiest way to provide fuel for your body as you reduce the number of carbs in your diet.

Omega-3, Omega-6, Omega-9

Omega-3 fatty acids are polyunsaturated fats that increase HDL cholesterol and improve heart health. They decrease the fat in the liver and improve liver function. These fats also reduce the inflammation in your body and organs. They are key in reducing waist size and promoting weight loss. Foods high in omega-3 fatty acids are walnuts and Chia seeds, or fish like salmon, mackerel, and sardines.

Omega-6 fatty acids are polyunsaturated fats that are used for energy. The problem is that most normal diets contain too much Omega-6. In large concentrations, these acids increase inflammation in the body and could cause associated diseases like asthma, rheumatoid arthritis, ulcerative colitis, and sinusitis. Omega-6 fatty acids must be consumed in moderation so that negative effects do not overwhelm the positive. Some of the foods high in omega-6 are soybean oil, corn oil, walnuts, almonds, and mayonnaise. Eating these foods in moderation will be the best way to receive the benefits of omega-6 fatty acids.

Omega-9 fatty acids are monounsaturated fats that are found naturally in the body but may be consumed as well. These fats are found to reduce inflammation and improve insulin sensitivity.

They may also improve metabolism when monounsaturated fats with omega-9 are consumed instead of saturated fats. Foods high in omega-9 are nut and seed oils like cashew oil, flaxseed oil, peanut oil, and olive oil. It is also found in olives as well as almonds, cashews, and walnuts. A moderate consumption of omega-9 fatty acids is appropriate because it is a natural part of the body's composition and it is well tolerated when ingested.

Foods with Omega-3 fatty acids should get added to your food plan two or three times a week. Omega-6 fatty acids should not be included in a grand way in the diet, while Omega-9 fatty acids are already found in the body, so it isn't necessary to work hard getting it into your system.

Fat Bombs

With all the talk about fats, let's not overlook fat bombs. Fat bombs are high-fat morsels of food used to boost fat levels while on the Keto diet. This is good if you find that you are not eating enough fat or feel hungry or lacking in energy. These items are high in fat, low in carbohydrates and combined into a small portion designed to boost energy, reduces cravings, and fill you up so you don't feel hungry. Because of the small size, do not overindulge. They are meant to be small bites that last. Pay attention to your macros, even while indulging in little bursts of food energy.

Chapter 5: What Macro Should I Aim For On The Keto Diet After 50?

Macronutrients are found in every food. They are the nutrients that fuel the body. Carbohydrates, proteins, and fats are included in the calories consumed and should be tracked while on the Keto diet. The information needed is on the nutritional value label found on foods. Accurately measure individual portions to be sure to have accurate nutritional information. These nutrients being tracked are typically called "macros" which is a shortened version of the word macronutrient. By adjusting the SKD (Standard Ketogenic Diet) and HPKD (High Protein Keto Diet), a gentler Keto plan may be created in order to fit the needs of women over 50.

First, we will look at the carbohydrates. You will be counting net carbs. Grams of net carbs are determined by subtracting the grams of dietary fiber and the grams of sugar alcohols from the grams of total carbohydrates. Dietary fiber does not release insulin into the body. The same is true of sugar alcohols. As a result, you will be able to eat more nutritionally dense foods and may satisfy your food cravings and hunger.

Next, we will look at fats. You will be eating 60 to 75% of your food as fat. This allows for a wide variety of foods, like bacon and pork rinds, to be included in your diet. Avocado, nuts, and other foods will be included in your diet as well. Because you will be eating food that is not processed, it will be important to eat healthy fats, including oil derived from natural food sources like avocado oil and coconut oil. High-quality butter and ghee will also be good sources of fat.

When we start to consider proteins, proteins do not need to be lean meats. In fact, the proteins included in Keto should be high in fat, since it will become our macro of preference. The Keto diet is only effective when there is a high amount of fat consumed.

Now, let's start calculating the macros. In order to calculate the grams of net carbohydrates to include in your daily diet, it is important to determine your body weight and then your percentage of body fat. To do this, weigh yourself. After determining your weight, divide your body weight by your height in inches and square height in inches squared. Multiply that by 703 and you will have your BMI, or body mass index.

Lbs/height in inches, squared, times 703=BMI. For example, if you are a 5-foot, 6-inch woman, weighing 200 lb that's, $200/66^2$ x 703=32.28. The BMI is 32.28.

Then calculate your body fat percentage. (1.2 x BMI) + (.23 * age) - 5.4 equals body fat percentage. When we plug in the BMI from our female example,

(1.2 * 32.28) + (.23*55) - 5.4 =45.98

So, the body fat percentage is 45.98%. Now that you have your body fat percentage take your body fat percentage and multiply it by your body weight. 45.98% x 200 lb. That equals 91.96 lbs of body fat. Subtract the body fat from your weight and you have your LBM (Lean Body Mass). So, 200 - 91.96 equals 108.04. The LBM is 108.04.

Now, it's time to determine the number of macronutrients to eat each day.

We can start with the calculation for protein. There are .8 grams per pound of lean body mass. In our example, .8* 108.04 equals 84 grams. This is equal to 346 calories because there are 4 calories in each gram of protein. In our example, 20% of the calories the daily calories will be from protein. Therefore, 346 calories/.20 equals 1730 total calories per day.

To determine the number of carbohydrates, let's look at the number of carbohydrates in a gentler Keto. 10% of the daily calories will come from carbs. 10% of 1730 calories is 173 calories. If you divide 173 calories by 4 (there are 4 calories in each carbohydrate), you will have 43.25g of carbohydrates as your daily allowance.

The remaining calories for each day will be fat calories:

346 Calories, Protein 86.50g   20%

    +173 Calories, Carbohydrate   43.25g   10%

519 Calories of Protein and Carbs

    -1730 (Total Daily Calories)

    1211 Calories, Fat   134.56g   70%

There are 9 calories in each fat gram. 1,211 calories/9 calories = 134.56g of fat for each day, or 70% of your daily calorie intake.

These macros will change as your BMI and LBM change. Make sure you adjust your macros every four or five weeks while you're losing weight so that your macros are accurate. You will want to record what you are eating and review your success in weight loss. This will allow you to track how your body is reacting to food combinations. Each body is different, and it is important to see how you feel when you are eating different foods and combinations of foods as your approach ketosis. Be sure you are eating whole grains and getting fiber through leafy green vegetables. You will also want to be remarkably familiar with nutrition labels to be sure you are not consuming hidden carbohydrates without realizing so.

Chapter 6: How Aging Affects Your Nutritional Needs

Our bodies change as we age. That makes our dietary needs change as well. Health flourishes with a correct nourishment and a sufficient water intake.

Dietary needs are distinctive for different people, ailments, action levels, and age. Nourishment gives us the vitality and supplements we need to remain sound.

Our bodies need protein (lentils, beans, tofu, spirulina, and various meat, dairy and fish), sugars (entire grains), solid fats (sound oils), nutrients, minerals, and water in order to properly function. Having a balanced diet may prevent some maladies, such as osteoporosis, hypertension, coronary illness, diabetes, and certain malignant growths.

Careful eating is significant after the age of 50. This implies contemplating all that you eat and drink. Set aside some effort to design your dinners, feast times and bites.

Tips for careful eating include:

- Pick an assortment of wide-ranging ingredients at every supper. This incorporates servings of organic products, vegetables, protein, and entire grains.

- Stay away from unfortunate calories such as cakes, treats, chips, and liquor.

- Watch serving sizes. Remember that a 3-ounce serving of meat is the size of a deck of cards. It's alright to get yourself chips every so often. Simply, don't thoughtlessly eat the chips from a pack while sitting in front of the TV. Measure out a fitting sum and set the pack aside.

- Purchase fresh, crisp, and colorful vegetables. This way, you will be keener to eat healthier.

- Add solid flavors to your nourishment if your preferences have changed.

- Figure out how to understand marks. Bundled things contain sustenance marks. These names mention to you what a serving is, the number of calories, absolute fat, cholesterol, sodium, sugars, and protein per serving.

Attempt to get the correct supplements in every dinner. Great supplements include:

- Calcium

- Day by day fiber (from nourishment)

- Nutrient A

- Nutrient C

Follow your primary care physician's guidance for sustenance. Not every person has the equivalent healthful needs after the age of 50. An individual who has diabetes may need to screen sugars first and calories second. An individual with hypertension may need to watch their sodium levels more than different supplements.

Additionally, not all supplements are equal. For instance, the calories in an organic product are more advantageous than the calories in a cake. The sugars in entire grains are more beneficial than those in candy.

People beyond 50 years old need various measures of calories every day. For instance:

- Dormant ladies ought to have 1,600 calories a day.

- Modestly dynamic ladies ought to have 1,800 calories a day.

- Dynamic ladies ought to have somewhere in the range of 2,000 and 2,200 calories a day.

- Truly latent men ought to have 2,000 calories a day.

- Reasonably dynamic men ought to have somewhere in the range of 2,200 and 2,400 calories a day.

- Dynamic men ought to have somewhere in the range of 2,400 and 2,800 calories a day.

Sanitation is another worry for people beyond 50 years old. As we age, our bodies are less ready to ward off diseases that originate from dangerous nourishment. Wash crude nourishments with cleanser.

Keep your hands, cutting apparatuses, and surface territories clean with hot lathery water while getting ready ingredients. Cook your food to the necessary temperature. What's more, consistently refrigerate nourishments inside 2 hours of cooking.

People beyond 50 years old need a lot of water. Specialists prescribe drinking water daily to forestall parchedness. Lack of hydration can prompt unsteadiness, falls, low pulse, poor kidney work, and different conditions. Drinking enough water enables your kidneys to flush the poisons from your body. Regardless of whether you are not parched, it's imperative to have water for the day. Plain water is ideal.

In any case, you can get water from soup juices and constrained measures of tea or espressos. But remember that an excessive amount of caffeine strips your waterway. Have a go at adding water to your daily practice by drinking a glass before every supper and bite, especially before breakfast. Taste it during dinners and bites as well. And last but not least, make certain to drink plenty of water before practicing or being out in the sun.

Chapter 7: Keto Food List

If you have made it this far, congratulations! This shows that you are fully ready to take on the Keto diet as a challenge and as a better lifestyle choice. I am happy that the information I offered proved useful, especially in your decision-making process. Now though, it is time for the technical aspect of the book, the food!

We will be looking into various sources of food which are deemed eligible or acceptable as a part of your Keto diet plan. It is imperative that you know exactly what type of food you are going to use while preparing your recipes. It must be an ingredient that compliments both your Keto plan and objective. Going for anything other than the approved food will end your run and you may have to start all over again.

Now, let's dive straight into the practical part. Let's discover all about food, what to eat, and what to say goodbye to. I will provide you with some great tips to help you with your selection, to ensure that you always end up with the finest quality and enjoy every ounce of the scrumptious recipes you will create using these food items.

I will provide you with some nutritional facts and we will eventually examine what exactly macros and calories are, and how we can keep track of all that is important.

The Richness within Keto

Food. Without it, we would be doomed. Keto, obviously, would fare no better either. But the presence of all the enormous types and kinds of food isn't exactly helping the case. For starters, we are not out to grab everything that packs a punch. We are more interested in food items that help our case and provide us with the specific nutrients we are seeking.

Remember, Keto is a high fat and low carb diet. When I say "low carb" I do really mean low; 20-50 grams of it in a day. That is quite a challenge for some.

It is important to remember the above and follow the guidelines set in place. With that said, let's move further ahead and see what kind of food items we can use.

The Good

Let me list down some of the healthiest Keto foods that you can get your hands on today from your local market. These do not cost much and add quite a bit of value and taste to your meal.

Seafood

Keto diet loves seafood, and that is as simple as that. Fish like salmon are packed with vitamin B and selenium, along with potassium too. The beauty behind it is that these are extremely low in carbs, so low that these are almost free of carbs in most cases. I did say *almost*, which is why it is best to keep a track of your carb intake.

When it comes to shellfish, the amount of carb varies. If you love crab or have a thing for shrimp, rejoice! These contain no carbs. For others, you may wish to double-check.

Now, since our daily limit for carbs consumption is rather tight, you may wish to start paying attention to the amount of carbs some of the shellfish have. A count for some popular ones is shown here (100 grams or 3.5 ounce):

- Mussels: 7 grams

- Oysters: 4 grams

- Clams: 5 grams

- Octopus: 4 grams

- Squid: 3 grams

Good news for those who love other fish like mackerel or sardines, these two, along with salmon, are extremely rich in omega-3 fats. As we mentioned before, various studies showed that fish intake can help with keeping your insulin level low and is good for your mental health.

Something for you to remember, twice a week is a good frequency.

Low Carb Veggies

They exist! They most certainly do and have been with us for a long time. The issue was that we never paid much attention to these. Time to find out which ones made it into the world of Keto.

Pretty much most non-starchy veggies are quite low in terms of carbs. They are significantly low in calories as well, but they do come with higher values when it comes to other nutrients. That would also include vitamin C in case you were looking for it!

The problem with vegetables and plants is that they come with fiber. Since our body doesn't exactly digest that, it often causes a bit of a miscalculation. To get the right values, try and seek out net carb count, which is essentially fiber deducted from the total carbs.

"So, it's okay to consume potatoes, then?" Not quite. You see, potatoes, yams, and beets contain starch, and just a single serving of these is enough to send your carbs count through the roof for the day. Keep a strict check on potatoes, as these are especially hard to avoid.

Vegetables also contain antioxidants which help by protecting us against free radicals that cause damage to our bodies. Broccoli, kale, and cauliflower also play a significant part in keeping heart issues and cancer at bay. All the more reasons for you to include veggies.

Cheese

Yes, please! Without cheese, we would be left in a world that is just tasteless in most cases. Cheese is delicious and nutritious as well. The best part is that all types of cheese are low in carbs and high in fats. It's like they were created with Keto in mind, or maybe the entire Keto diet was created by someone who preferred cheese. Either way, it's a win-win for us all.

While cheese is high in saturated fats, there are no such studies to show that it is bad for our health overall, and that is good news for everyone.

Contrary to popular belief, cheese contains what are called conjugated linoleic acids. In simple English, it is a fat that helps with fat loss, which is odd - nonetheless helpful.

Avocado

Hands down, the finest ingredient of the lot. Use it on its own or mix it with various food items, and you will always get that great sensation, a punch of great taste, and great nutritional values.

For every 100 grams of avocados, roughly around one-half of a medium-sized avocado, you only get nine grams of carbs. If that raised some curiosity, here's another fact: seven of those grams are fiber. That means you are only consuming two grams of carbs. That is just phenomenal.

They hold a high dose of important vitamins and minerals, and the high level of potassium makes everything a little easier during the transition to Keto.

Mmm... Meat and Poultry!

Of course, meals are never considered complete without meat and poultry. The good news is that you have a diverse range of these available as good Keto food. The only catch is that you must buy your meat and poultry fresh.

Fresh meat and poultry are free from carbs and contain high vitamin B counts. They are loaded with potassium, zinc, and selenium too, and that further helps our case.

However, the main reason we go for these is protein, as they will help us in preserving our muscle mass throughout the low carb diet.

When choosing your meat, opt for grass-fed meat. This option is safe and comes with all the goodness we seek.

Eggs

Cheap, easy to make, and delicious when cooked right. Eggs are one of the most versatile foods on the face of planet Earth.

To give you an idea of how great these are, one large egg only holds less than one gram of carbs and six grams of protein. That, then, makes eggs as the ideal food for anyone following the Ketogenic diet.

Studies have shown that eggs trigger the release of hormones which give us a feeling of fullness while keeping our blood sugar levels intact. When consuming eggs, ensure you eat the yolk as well, to get the most nutrients.

Now I know, some may be quick to point out that yolks contain high cholesterol, but the fact is that these do not raise cholesterol levels in most people. However, to make things easier, consult your doctor first to find out if you can consume eggs regularly.

Nuts and Seeds

No talk about protein is ever complete without the mention of nuts and seeds. Those who are comfortable in consuming these are in for a treat.

To provide you an idea of just how much these offer, here is a list of some common nuts and seeds and their carb values (28 grams or 1 ounce):

- Almonds - 3 grams

- Brazil nuts - 1 gram

- Cashews - 8 grams

- Chia Seeds - 1 gram

- Flaxseeds - 0 grams

- Macadamia nuts - 2 grams

- Pecans - 1 gram

- Pistachios - 5 grams

- Pumpkin Seeds - 4 grams

- Sesame seeds - 3 grams

- Walnuts - 2 grams

Other Food Items

Frankly, this list continues to grow almost every year. However, to give you a quick view of what you can expect to eat, here are some other food items included and considered genuinely good within the Keto circle.

- Coconut Oil

- Olive Oil

- Plain Greek Yogurt

- Cottage Cheese

- Berries

- Butter and Cream

- Shirataki Noodles

- Olives

- Unsweetened Coffee

- Unsweetened Tea

- Dark Chocolate

- Cocoa Powder

Now let's see what you should *avoid* while observing the Keto diet!

Chapter 8: Foods to Avoid When On Keto Diet After 50

I will show you the kinds of food you want to avoid at all costs. As we mentioned before, you will need to avoid high-carbs food. Of course, many of them are healthy, but they just contain too many carbs. Here is a list of common food you should limit or avoid altogether.

Bread and Grains

Breads are a staple food in many countries. You have loaves, bagels, tortillas, and the list goes on. However, no matter what form bread takes, it still packs a lot of carbs.

Depending on your daily carb limit, eating a sandwich or bagel can put you way across the line. So, if you really want to eat bread, it is best to bake Keto variants at home instead. And remember that grains such as rice, wheat, and oats pack a lot of carbs, so limit or avoid them as well.

Fruits

Fruits are healthy for you. In fact, they have been linked to a lower risk of heart disease and cancer. However, there are a few that you need to avoid in your Keto diet. And that is because some of those foods, such as banana, raisins, dates, mango and pear, pack quite a lot of carbs.

As a general rule, avoid sweet and dried fruits. Berries are an exception because they do not contain as much sugar and are rich in fiber and antioxidants. This means that you can still eat some of them (around 50 grams) but remember that moderation is key.

Vegetables

Vegetables are just as healthy for your body. Most of the Keto diet does not care about how many vegetables you eat, as long as they are low in starch. Vegetables that are rich in fiber can help with weight loss. For one, they make you feel full for longer, since they help suppress your appetite. Another benefit is that your body will burn more calories to break and digest them. Moreover, they help control blood sugar and aid with your bowel movements.

But remember to avoid or limit vegetables that are high in starch because they have more carbs than fiber. That includes corn, potato, sweet potato, and beets.

Pasta

Pasta is also a staple food in many countries. It is versatile and convenient. As with any other convenient food, pasta is rich in carbs. So, when you are on your Keto diet, spaghetti or any other types of pasta are not recommended. You will probably think that you can get away with it by eating a small portion, but that is not our case.

Thankfully, that does not mean you need to give up on it altogether. If you are craving pasta, you can try some other alternatives that are low in carbs such as spiralized veggies or shirataki noodles.

Cereal

Cereal is also a huge offender because sugary breakfast cereals pack a lot of carbs. That also applies to "healthy cereals". Just because they use other words to describe their product does not mean that you should believe them. That also applies to oatmeal, whole-grain cereals, etc.

Thus, when you eat a bowl of cereal when you are doing Keto, you are already way over your carb limit, and we haven't even added milk into the equation! Therefore, avoid whole-grain cereal or cereals that we mention here altogether.

Beer

In reality, you can drink most alcoholic beverages in moderation without fear. For instance, dry wine does not have that many carbs and hard liquor has no carbs at all. So, you can drink them without worry. However, beer is an exception to this rule because it packs a lot of carbs.

Carbs in beers or other liquid are considered to be liquid carbs and they are even more dangerous than solid carbs. You see, when you eat food that is rich in carbs, you at least feel full. When you drink liquid carbs, you do not feel full as quickly, so the appetite suppression effect is little.

Sweetened Yogurt

Yogurt is actually allowed, since it does not have that many carbs. It is a very versatile food to have in your Keto diet. The problem comes when you consume yogurt variants that are rich in carbs such as fruit-flavored, low-fat, sweetened, or nonfat yogurt. A single serving of sweetened yogurt contains as many carbs as a single serving of dessert.

If you really love yogurt, you can get away with half a cup of plain Greek yogurt with 50 grams of raspberries or blackberries.

Juice

Fruit juices are perhaps the worst beverage you can put into your system when you are on a Keto diet. One may argue that juice provides some nutrients, but the problem is that it contains a lot of carbs that are too easy to digest. As a result, your blood sugar level will spike whenever you drink it. That also applies to vegetable juice because of the fast-digesting carbs present.

And, like we just said, the brain does not process liquid carbs the same way as solid carbs. Solid carbs can help suppress appetite, but liquid carbs will only put your appetite into overdrive.

Low-fat and fat-free salad dressings

As previously mentioned, fruits and vegetables are largely okay, as long as they are low in carbs. But if you *must* buy salads, keep in mind that commercial dressings pack more carbs than you think, especially the fat-free and low-fat variants.

So, if you want to enjoy your salad, try using a creamy, full-fat dressing instead. To really cut down on carbs, you can use vinegar and olive oil, both of which are proven to help with heart health and aid with weight loss.

Beans and Legumes

These are also very nutritious as they are rich in fiber. Research has shown that eating them has many health benefits such as reduced inflammation and heart disease risk.

However, they are also rich in carbs. You may be able to enjoy a small amount of them when you are on your Keto diet, but make sure you know exactly how much you can eat before you exceed your carb limit.

Sugar

We mean sugar in any form, including honey. As you probably know, foods that contain lots of sugar - such as cookies, candies, and cake - are forbidden on a Keto diet or any other form of diet that is designed to lose weight.

What you may not be aware of is that nature's sugars, such as honey, are just as rich in carbs as processed sugar. In fact, natural forms of sugar contain even more carbs.

Not only is that sugar rich in carbs, it also adds little to no nutritional value to your meal. When you are on a Keto diet, you need to keep in mind that you should favor food that is nutritious and rich in fiber. So sugar is out of the question!

If you really want to sweeten your food, you can just use a healthy sweetener instead because they do not add as many carbs.

Chips and Crackers

These two are some of the most popular snacks. What some people do not realize is that one packet of chips contains several servings and should not be all eaten in one go. The carbs can add up very quickly if you do not watch what you eat.

Crackers also pack a lot of carbs, although the amount varies based on how they are made. But even whole-wheat crackers contain a lot of carbs.

Due to how processed snacks are produced, it is difficult to stop yourself from finishing the pack within a short period of time. Therefore, it is advised that you avoid them altogether.

Milk

I previously mentioned that cereal contains a lot of carbs and a breakfast cereal will put you way over your carbs limit. But that's without you even adding milk. Milk also contains a lot of carbs on its own. Therefore, avoid it if you can, even though it is a good source of many nutrients such as calcium, potassium, and other B vitamins.

Of course, that does not mean that you have to ditch milk altogether. You can get away with a tablespoon or two of milk for your coffee, however cream or half-and-half is better if you drink coffee frequently. These two contain very few carbs. If you really love to drink milk in large amounts or need it to make your favorite drinks, consider using coconut milk or unsweetened almond milk instead.

Gluten-free baked goods

Wheat, barley, and rye all contain gluten. Some people who have celiac disease still want to enjoy these delicacies but are unable to, because their gut will become inflamed in response to gluten. As such, gluten-free variants have been created to cater to their needs.

Gluten-free diets are extremely popular nowadays, but what many people don't seem to realize is that they pack quite a lot of carbs. That includes gluten-free bread, muffins, and other baked products. In reality, they contain even more carbs than their glutenous variant. Moreover, the flour used to make these gluten-free products is made from grains and starches. So, when you consume a gluten-free bread, your blood sugar level spikes. Just stick to whole foods. Alternatively, you can use almond or coconut flour to make your own low-carb bread.

Chapter 9: Keto Side Effects and How to Solve Them

Everybody is praising the special Keto diet, as it gives prominent results in the weight loss procedure. But before starting the Keto diet, you should be aware of the side effects caused by it so you can decide whether it is fine for you or not.

The truth is that all types of diet have negative effects to start with because your body has gotten used to the bad habits. Once you make the shift to a more positive way of eating, the body sort of goes on a rebellious phase so it feels like everything is going wrong. For example, a person who used to eat lots of sugar in a day can have severe headaches once they start avoiding it. This is a withdrawal symptom, and it tells you that your diet is actually making positive changes to the body – albeit it takes a little bit of patience on your part.

So, what can one expect when they make that change towards a healthy Ketogenic Diet? Here are some of the things to expect and of course – how to troubleshoot these problems.

Long Term Side Effects

A study titled "Metabolic Effects of the Very Low Carbohydrate Diets: Misunderstood Villains of Human Metabolism" shows that for short-term purposes, the Ketogenic Diet is highly effective. It lets you burn all that excess fat quickly, but in a healthy way. However, if you do this for a long period of time, there will be side effects. For example, there can be muscle loss, dizziness, kidney problems, acidosis, and focusing problems. Does that mean you shouldn't go on a Ketogenic Diet at all? Of course not! This only means that you'll have to be careful when using this diet. Don't push it too hard and you will be able to get all the positive results with none of the downsides!

Do you know why a low carbohydrate diet is bad if done for a long time? Well, balance is important in anything you do, and the Ketogenic Diet doesn't really support balance. If you get rid of an entire food group for a long period of time, your body will rebel against you. Remember – the Ketogenic Diet relies on stored fat in your body. If there is no more stored fat, it really won't work anymore so you will have to increase your carbohydrates. To solve this problem, I recommend going on a 30-day Ketogenic Diet first and assessing your health before moving forward. Asking your doctor what to do "next" after the 30-day plan or after hitting your weight goal is also a good idea. Personally, I decided to increase my carbohydrate intake slightly after hitting my goal weight.

Keto-flu

The Keto Flu is the most prominent problem you'll encounter when starting the diet. It's a perfectly normal reaction by the body that may seem alarming because, well, the symptoms don't really feel good. The reason why Keto-flu occurs is that, when the body switches from high carb intake to low carb intake, the insulin level in the body lowers. As a result, ketosis occurs. It takes time for your body and brain to adapt to these changes.

You have to understand, your body has been running on a specific type of gasoline for years. It's been taking fuel from sugar, and with the Ketogenic Diet, it's like you're changing your fuel source to a cleaner and more sustainable type. It makes sense that the engine growls a little in protest – but after that, you'll be able to run beautifully without the guilt.

The Keto Flu has the following symptoms:

- Headaches

- Fatigue

- Irritability

- Brain fog or difficulty focusing

- Motivational problems

- Sugar cravings

- Dizziness

- Nausea

- Muscle cramps

- Frequent urination

These symptoms are all heavily dependent on the kind of person doing the Keto Diet. Since you're already in our 50s, the symptoms may be more prominent, especially if you rely heavily on carbohydrates in your diet. However, if you eat mostly low-carb food, these effects may not be as obvious.

But how do you solve them? Here are some of the best way to get rid of the Keto Flu as quickly as possible!

First, increase your water and salt consumption.

I know I've already mentioned salt and water, but it really is important!

In the first week of the Keto diet, there is a gradual change of the fluid balance in the body. As the body starts to use its stored sugar in the form of glycogen, water is released as well, and pushed out of the body through urine. When the fluids pass out, the body salt also gets depleted, often resulting in an excessive loss of salt while maintaining the state of ketosis.

Also, you may not notice it, but a lot of the salt you consume is through carbohydrates like bread, pasta, rice, and so on. Salt tends to make you thirsty so if you eat little salt, you're also less likely to look for water during the day.

What happens now? Every time you feel dizzy or tired or nauseous while on a Keto Diet, just dissolve salt in water and gulp it down. Now, this is not going to taste good - but I promise that it will help you feel better. You can always try consuming the salt and water separately – whatever you find most convenient. Beef stock, bone broth, or chicken stock are also great alternatives and tastier too! As for water, try to hit a target of 3 liters of water every day. The good news is that this doesn't have to be plain water – your smoothies, coffee, and tea drinks are also counted.

Magnesium and potassium are also important electrolytes to add to your diet. You can get them from natural foods such as almond, hazelnuts and walnuts, as well as soybean sprouts and spinach.

Add more fat in your diet. Do you still think that fat is the enemy? Hopefully, together we learned that this is not so true, especially during Keto! While on this diet, it makes sense to eat lots of fats especially if your carbohydrate intake dips to an all-time low. If you lower the carbohydrate consumption without an equal fat increase, then you will always feel hungry and tired.

Don't be impatient – go slower. Remember what we said about the body changing fuels when you're switching to the Ketogenic Diet? Well, the changing process doesn't have to be overnight. Choose to convert one meal at a time to a Keto-friendly set instead of changing all of them on your first day. Just remember – the Keto Flu *will* pass, so the first few days of discomfort should not discourage you in the slightest. If you want to minimize the trouble, try starting your Ketogenic Diet on a low-stress period – like a holiday. So basically, instead of eating less than 50 grams of carbohydrates a day, you can have a target of 50 to 70.

Do NOT count calories or restrict your food consumption. When it comes to the Ketogenic Diet – you don't have to calorie count. Again, you don't want to stuff yourself with food just because you don't have to count calories, but the truth is calories do not matter so much when your body is at a state of ketosis. It doesn't matter so much how many you're getting – your body will *always* break down the fat deposits and there will be weight loss. It is recommended to notice the calorie intake – especially in the beginning - but not to be obsessive about it! Stressing about the calorie intake or depriving yourself of food because of the calories can actually worsen the symptoms of Keto Flu and will make it more difficult for you to stick to the diet. The bottom line is this: as long as you're eating the allowed food items in allowed portions, then you're OK.

Limit your physical activity. That's the good news when first starting the Ketogenic Diet – you don't have to exercise. If you're health-conscious, then chances are you do light walks on a routine basis. That's perfectly OK – as long as you don't over-exert yourself. Now, there will be days when you will actually feel too good. Like you can go out and exercise because you have all this extra energy. When this happens, resist the temptation to do too much too soon. Your body is already burning as much fat as it can – don't push it too hard during the first phase or you might get sick. If you're restless, try doing yoga, light walking, or just stretching.

Take some supplements. People who use the Ketogenic Diet for a long time may also have vitamin and mineral deficiency. It's not easily obvious but it could happen, so you'll have to be prepared. The usual vitamins and minerals lacking in a Ketogenic Diet include calcium, zinc, selenium, and vitamin D – so try taking a multivitamin during your diet. Again, I can't stress this enough: always consult your doctor before taking any sort of medication. This is especially true if you have pre-existing health problems and are also taking medication for maintenance.

Ketosis

Ketosis is a process in which the body converts the stored fat into energy and produces ketones as a by-product, which helps in maintaining a fast-metabolic state. This process is used to facilitate the weight loss strategy. The energy source that comes from carbohydrates is diverted and the body starts to use body fat, resulting in fat loss.

People with diabetes experience ketosis, as the body doesn't make enough insulin to process the glucose in the body. If this hormone's level is too low, we can find ketone bodies in urines, while usually, they are only present in small percentages.

When the process of ketosis starts, a person starts to feel temporary side effects such as headaches, fatigue, brain fog, irritation, troubled sleep, nausea, stomach-aches, dizziness, sugar cravings, etc.

Ketoacidosis

People, especially those with diabetes, need to monitor their ketone level with much care. Having too many ketones in the body can lead to ketoacidosis, due to the poisoning that they cause inside the body. Because of its rapid development, it's not something that should be taken lightly. The illness causes a high level of hormonal changes, which will eventually start to work against insulin. Some early symptoms include abdominal pain, flushed or dry skin, confused concentration, dry mouth, urination, vomiting, nausea, etc.

Constipation or Diarrhea

These problems are fairly common because, well, you're changing your diet! Your body will react one way or another. Make sure you get enough fluids in your system and taking natural supplements which are available through many stores. You can also try taking laxatives that are made especially without carbohydrates, in case of constipation.

Water consumption:

This is important in both cases. While diarrhea causes dehydration, dehydration is the cause of constipation. So, one of the remedies is definitely increasing the water intake. In this way – by rehydrating your body - you will attenuate the dryness that has been caused by diarrhea or that caused the constipation in the first place.

Fiber intake:

Fibers are very important when it comes to the health of our digestive system. It's usually recommended to have plenty of vegetables in our diet, since they are one of the best sources of fiber. These macros help the intestine work properly, resulting in a reduced risk of constipation. On contrary, avoid fibers if you are suffering with diarrhea, since they can further irritate the intestines!

As a general rule, if alarming symptoms occurs while you're on the Ketogenic Diet, I want you to consult your doctor ASAP! Again, reactions may vary from one person to the next and I don't want you shrugging off certain symptoms as if they're just "part" of the diet. Stay motivated but also be mindful of what is happening to your body. Remember – we want you to be healthy!

Keto Rash

Prurigo pigmentosa, known as "Keto rash", is another rare side effect of the Keto diet. It is an inflammatory condition of the skin and typical symptoms include redness of the skin, itchy rashes around the neck and truck, papules (red spots), rash on abdomen, and a dark brown pattern after the disappearance of spots. It is a type of dermatitis and, according to research, it is more common in Asian woman.

Researchers cannot be entirely certain about the exact reason or cause for the Keto rash, but few thought it could be related to some associated conditions like Sjogren's syndrome, still's disease, and H. Pylori infection. Still, it's called Keto rash because of the strong correlation between the apparition of these rashes and the presence of ketones in the body.

A few of the treatments include:

Carbohydrate intake

If you think your change in diet, or switching to Keto caused you the rash, try to bring carbohydrates back into your diet. This will help you to ease the inflammation. If you do not want to compromise your Keto diet, then go for more moderate low-carb options instead.

Nutritional deficiency

Deficiency of some nutrients can also cause rashes. Deficiency of vitamin B-12, Vitamin A, and C are directly linked to acute skin conditions. While having a moderate diet, there is a possibility that your body is not getting the right amount of the minerals and vitamins that you need. Try to have colorful fruits and vegetables in your diet to complete your deficiencies.

Skincare

Maybe you have a sensitive skin type, which can detect the changes in your body and be affected by them more than normal. Take care of your skin as much as possible. Use cleansers, gentle soaps, and lukewarm water when you take baths.

Kidney and Heart Damage

As the urination increases during this type of diet, the level of electrolytes like magnesium, sodium, and potassium decrease. In some cases, this might lead to acute injuries of the kidney. Dehydration may result in serious conditions like kidney stones, kidney injury or light-headedness. Also, for a normal beating of the heart, electrolytes are necessary. In order to avoid this type of problems, a proper diet has to be followed. So, be careful and take the needed precautions.

Cramps in Legs

Cramps in legs are common when you switch to a low-carb diet. It is a minor issue, but it can also be painful. It is mainly caused by the loss of minerals you could face, especially magnesium and potassium. There are simple ways to avoid this pain:

- Drink water and maintain your salt intake.

- Use a magnesium supplement if needed.

Bad Breath

While following a strict Keto diet, some people observed a change in their breath, often described as the smell of nail polish remover or acetone. This smell is actually a good sign. It means that your body is burning a lot of fat and producing ketones to fuel your organs.

To avoid bad breath, observe proper oral hygiene along with a good intake of water. You can also use breath fresheners and other products.

Energy Loss

Another misconception regarding Keto diet is that glucose is the best energy source. When in reality, maintaining an appropriate level of energy is way more challenging while having a standard diet, as it fluctuates according to the food intake and blood sugar level.

You may feel that your energy level is low at the beginning of this diet. This happens because your body is adapting – but it's temporary and it will adjust after a week or two, so do not worry.

Chapter 10: Fitness and Exercise: How to Lose Weight and Alleviate the Symptoms of Menopause

The first aspect that we have seen so far is nutrition. We say that a woman tends to consume less. The first thing you have to do is reduce the kcal that we have introduced. Try to keep a food diary for a week, record each meal and relative grams, then include everything in a nutritional application and try to reduce the kcals by 5-10% next week.

See how it works out and if the weight doesn't move, reduce it by another 5-10% so you can reach the desired weight. We come to the second aspect, which is related to training. In this case, women must avoid all activities that can inflame.

Therefore, avoid many repetitions, limit yourself to working with 3 series for each muscle group, 8 to 15 repetitions coming to feel muscle fatigue at the end of each series. This work will enable you to increase muscle tone without inflaming yourself locally and systemically. Our advice is to exercise at least 2-3 times a week for 45-60 minutes to lose weight during menopause. The first thing you need to know: You need to determine what your goals are. This point is quite basic: each physical activity has different characteristics and allows you to achieve different results.

Gymnastic activities with little consideration often produce results and tasks without stopping. What are the main goals you need to have in your physical activity plan? I would say at least 3:

- help you burn more calories, keeping the cardiovascular system in shape

- help you strengthen the tissues that weaken most, i.e. MUSCLE and BONE

- Help you prevent or solve problems typical of this phase, i.e. muscle pain, arthrosis.

Let's be clear right away: there is NO SINGLE activity that can make you achieve ALL these goals SIMULTANEOUSLY. You need a particular type of activity for each of these goals, and I will now explain just what type of activity. If for reasons of time or others you will not be able to do everything, you shouldn't worry too much, but at least you will know the reason why you will not be reaching a certain goal! In short, if you hoped that "an hour of walking + going to dance on Saturday evening" would have an invigorating effect for the muscles, prepare for a small (or big!) Disappointment.

One of the most desired and sought-after goals through physical activity is that of slimming. Losing weight is also one of the most "missed" objectives by the various users. The reason is simple: burning calories with physical activity is hard and time consuming, while consuming many with nutrition is easy, painless and even pleasant. To help you with physical activity, you need something that allows you to burn a good number of calories.

Keep in mind that to lose fat, you need to take, on average, about 300 calories less per day than you consume. In an hour of walking at "medium" pace, you consume between 100 and 200 calories. And here is why, for most people, the famous "walks" do not have a significant impact on fat: to have a slimming effect, you should walk at least a couple of hours a day in a row. Walking is relaxing and is good for the cardiovascular system, but if your goal is to lose weight ... do your math well!

To get an idea, here is the "average" calorie consumption of various activities, calculated on an hour of activity and for a woman weighing 60 kg: if your weight is greater, keep in mind that consumption increases.

Remember: around 300 calories per day, so around 2000 calories per week. That's why "it's tough", and that's why you can't leave the diet behind.

- Aerobics course: 300 kcal / hour

- Medium speed exercise bike: 400 kcal / hour

- Swimming: around 500 kcal / hour

- Gardening: around 300 Kcal per hour

Physical activity strengthens muscles and bones

Other changes that women hate? There is clearly muscle loss, especially in the arms and legs. Can this muscle be restored? And how? And what can be done about osteoporosis? So, the answers to these questions are- yes, but it's not easy. The reason is simple and to understand it, just focus on these two simple concepts:

- Muscles develop and tone only when requested by our body

- Bones follow the same principle, that is, the more they strain, the stronger they become. To tighten muscles and strengthen bones, you need activities that burden you.

Of course, they must be progressive and controlled overloads. Consequently, activities such as swimming, walking, or cycling will not help you much: the overload (which is not fatigue, be careful!) To which the muscles are subjected is minimal. In fact, the only activity that allows you to strengthen muscles and strengthen bones is physical activity in the gym.

Physical activity in the gym: recommendations

Physical activity in the gym should overload your muscles: Muscles will "register" and "adapt" to these new needs, will be strengthened. For this to happen, weighing a kilo and twisting with a stick are certainly not enough. Ask the trainer for a special muscle strengthening program.

Physical activity to prevent or treat various problems

Menopausal women who don't have to deal with back or neck pain are counted on the fingers of one hand. Among other things, this problem often complicates physical activity: it is very difficult to lift weights when you suffer from back pain!

Therefore, part of your physical activity plan should aim to increase muscle and joint elasticity.

In this case, targeted stretches are extraordinary activities that you can do with other sports, among them. When you visit the gym, let your trainer show you some exercise on important points, or contact a physiotherapist for professional advice. Conclusion: What physical activity should I choose?

I'll say it again, one activity is not enough to reach all goals. As a result, it is not easy to achieve certain goals. It would be ideal to schedule activities throughout the day and throughout the week to cover all different aspects, but most people do not have time. So, it's better to focus on what seems to be your main goal:

- Do you want to lose fat? As you have seen, you have to grind kilometers!

- Do you want to tone your muscles? Now you know that you have no alternative to the gym!

- Do you want to solve the ailments first? Devote yourself to stretching and stretching, perhaps with the help of a professional.

I understand that you may not like reading certain information: maybe you hate gyms, or you thought that walking half an hour in the evening could have positive effects on losing weight. Let's find out: Exercise is recommended, but certainly not an obligation! Now you know what physical activity is needed to achieve certain goals.

Chapter 11: Tips for Organizing a Work Program from the Age Of 50

There is never a need to start exercising. But remember that regular activity is necessary to stay healthy and to avoid recurring illnesses such as heart disease, obesity, and diabetes. If you've never exercised before, it can be challenging to get started. But it has been proven that starting a work program later in life has a wide range of benefits, such as boosting heart health. Here is how you can begin to introduce exercising in your life, after the age of 50.

Find your motivation

First things first; *why* do you want to start working out? Perhaps you are quite busy with your job and you hope to take a break, or you may want to stay tuned to your grandchildren longer. Finding your reason for being more active will help you remain true to your intention. It will soon become a part of your life and you will certainly notice how good it feels to be active!

Keep it regular

This is called a *routine* for a reason. When it comes to exercises for the crowd of 50 and over, doctors recommend at least 30 minutes of moderate to vigorous aerobic activity - such as brisk walking and muscle building - at least two days a week. Have you opted for ski training? Try to find a fun way to remain active and stay motivated!

Start slowly

The truth is that you may not be able to start as quickly as you think, so if you are trying to start a workout for the first time, focus on low-intensity exercises that will not get you injured. To start, try a few workouts at home, then slowly transition to light weight training at the gym, yoga, or more intensive training. Try to wait at least 48 hours between training the same muscle group. This will allow your body to recover and find strength again. If you feel like something's wrong, don't neglect it.

Try a variety of activities

Experiment a little with different types of training and find what works best for you. Join a club and try the various forms of fitness they offer. You can certainly find the one for you! You could try going for a bike path, hiking, taking a Zumba class, or try something you always wanted to try, but never did. Experts say it is good to focus on a combination of strength training, stamina training, flexibility and balance training. This way, you will be entirely in shape!

Keep a food log

It is a good idea to keep track of your eating habits, when you are first starting this diet. This way, you will easily notice which ingredients to reduce and which ones you should be getting more of! By writing down what you are eating on a daily basis, you will easily understand the details of your diet and you might even see some mistakes you never noticed before. You don't necessarily have to count every calorie, in order to succeed. You should only do it in the beginning to estimate the quantities you need. Then, when you will know your eating habits better, you can just follow our recipes without all the counting!

Chapter 12: How to Stay Motivated During Weight Loss

Weight loss requires motivation. Among the thousands of people who undergo the process of weight loss, only a few obtain and maintain the desired results. The causes of this phenomenon are truly diverse. You must have the courage to distinguish between the true cause and the alibi. We should be able to find the right motivation when starting a new diet. The right reason means something that can actually keep us following all the steps in this program. It must be a positive thought that can keep us active, in order to increase your chances of success. Let's learn to use our mind the right way (what motivates you? And what makes you happy?) and we will understand how we can combine fitness and weight loss with our interests and value systems for long-term success.

The "fundamental why"

To find our inner motivation and start with the right foot, we must find the root cause that drives us, the fundamental "why".

We have to find ways to focus on being happy and in shape, rather than just losing weight and trying on swimsuits for the summer. It sounds basic, but positive thinking is something you must pick up if you want to pursue a weight loss or fitness program successfully.

We should sit with pen and paper and write down why do we want to follow the program. Write alle the reasons that come to mind, even the most trivial ones. Let's analyze our answers.

What is the reason? Is this external or internal motivation? Even if it's internal, do they agree with our values? For example, if one of our answers is similar to one of the following:

- Because I have to.

- Because I'm ashamed of my weight.

- Because I want to be skinny for the summer.

That means our motivation is external.

But is external motivation bad? It's not easy answering this question. The easiest answer is yes, external motivation is not beneficial in the long run. Still, many studies show that such motivation is quite common at the beginning of the weight-loss path.

Those studies have shown that external motivation was quite helpful in the initial stages of nutrition, while a long-term success was held by those who could find an intrinsic motivation. So, we understand that an external motivation can still produce results, but only in the short term - and as we know, weight loss is a long-term problem.

External motivation is positive as long as it's not the only type of motivation we have!

Discover intrinsic motivation

What answers can we look for to find our intrinsic motivation? What can we think of, that will get us to obtain the results we are hoping for? The answers must be inherent to who we are as individuals, our values, and our lifestyle. We can be adventurous, or some aspects of friendship can be important to us. Whatever it is, we must look for things that really respect our value structure. We can now be truly clear about what makes us happy and what is fundamental to us, or we can only have vague ideas about it, but we don't know how to use these values to lose weight. In this case, there are simple exercises to help us find out what is actually important to us and help us understand our specific guidelines.

Our best proof

We should think of a time when we felt our best, when we were proud of ourselves. What were we doing? Who were we with? This memory is like a snapshot that portrays us in our best pose. It doesn't matter if it's a big or a small thing, as long as it represents us and our character. Let's write down this event in detail and then reflect. What does this event mean, compared to what gives value to our life? What does it say about our strengths? And what do we like to do just for the sake of doing it? Ask yourself:

- Why did I choose this event?

- Why is it significant for me?

- What does it symbolize or represent?

This exercise will help us get in touch with what really interests us and will help us improve our health, by working on what is meaningful to us, showing what our personal guides are. For example, this exercise could reveal to us that we are people for whom family is the most important value. In this case, we could think of the "fundamental why" in terms of loved ones and connect them with our health goals. We could go to the gym with our partner or go for a walk with our parents. It could also describe to us that what we define as important is to always to have goals for improvement. In this case, defining new goals is something that can drive us and help us succeed. Maybe we could register for the next marathon!

It could reveal that the moment we feel the best is when we can use humor and be playful. If so, we may want to consider harnessing this energy when it's time to decide which fitness classes to sign up for. In fact, for some people, the mere fact of wearing funny socks in the gym can change their attitude towards training. The basic idea of this exercise is to understand what interests us naturally, in order to use these resources to create lifestyle changes that are pleasant and therefore not too tiring to maintain in the long run.

Chapter 13: 28 Days Meal Plan

Days	Breakfast	Lunch/Dinner	Snacks
1	Delicious Poached Eggs	Salmon Skewers	Marinated Eggs
2	Keto Breakfast Bowl	Coconut Salmon with Napa Cabbage	Sausage and Cheese Dip
3	Yummy Eggs and Sausages	Keto Tuna Casserole	Tasty Onion and Cauliflower Dip
4	Breakfast Scrambled Eggs	Baked Fish Fillets with Vegetables in Foil	Pesto Crackers
5	Delicious Frittata	Fish & Chips	Pumpkin Muffins
6	Smoked Salmon Breakfast	Baked Salmon with Almonds and Cream Sauce	Taco Flavored Cheddar Crisps
7	Feta and Asparagus Delight	Shrimp and Sausage Bake	Keto Seed Crispy Crackers
8	Special Breakfast Eggs	Herb Butter Scallops	Parmesan Crackers
9	Eggs Baked In Avocados	Pan Seared Halibut with Citrus Butter Sauce	Deviled Eggs
10	Shrimp and Bacon Breakfast	Baked Coconut Haddock	Almond Garlic Crackers
11	Holiday Morning Bread	Classic Pork Tenderloin	Chocolate Mug Muffin
12	Masterpiece Bread	Signature Italian Pork Dish	Almond Cookies
13	Dense Morning Bread	Flavor Packed Pork Loin	Pumpkin Pie Cupcakes
14	Multi Seeds Bread	Spiced Pork Tenderloin	Brownies
15	Sandwich Bread	Sticky Pork Ribs	Ice Cream

16	Magic Cheese Bread	Valentine's Day Dinner	Cheesecake Keto Fat Bombs
17	10-Minutes Bread	South East Asian Steak Platter	Keto Egg Crepes
18	Subtle Rosemary Bread	Pesto Flavored Steak	Keto Naan
19	Brunch Time Bread	Flawless Grilled Steak	Peanut Butter Cookies
20	Amazing Cheddar Bread	Mongolian Beef	Buttery Keto Crepes
21	Delicious Poached Eggs	Salmon Skewers	Marinated Eggs
22	Keto Breakfast Bowl	Coconut Salmon with Napa Cabbage	Sausage and Cheese Dip
23	Yummy Eggs and Sausages	Keto Tuna Casserole	Tasty Onion and Cauliflower Dip
24	Breakfast Scrambled Eggs	Baked Fish Fillets with Vegetables in Foil	Pesto Crackers
25	Delicious Frittata	Fish & Chips	Pumpkin Muffins
26	Smoked Salmon Breakfast	Baked Salmon with Almonds and Cream Sauce	Taco Flavored Cheddar Crisps
27	Feta and Asparagus Delight	Shrimp and Sausage Bake	Keto Seed Crispy Crackers
28	Special Breakfast Eggs	Herb Butter Scallops	Parmesan Crackers

Chapter 14: Breakfast Recipes

1. Delicious Poached Eggs.

Preparation time: 10 minutes

Cooking time: 35 minutes

Servings: 4

Ingredients

6 eggs

1 tablespoon ghee

1 Serrano pepper, chopped

1 red bell pepper, chopped

3 tomatoes, chopped

1 white onion, chopped

3 garlic cloves, minced

1 teaspoon paprika

1 teaspoon cumin

¼ teaspoon chili powder

1 tablespoon cilantro, chopped

Salt and black pepper to the taste

Directions

Heat up a pan with the ghee over medium heat, add onion, stir and cook for 10 minutes.

Add Serrano pepper and garlic, stir and cook for 1 minute.

Add red bell pepper, stir and cook for 10 minutes.

Add tomatoes, salt, pepper, chili powder, cumin and paprika, stir and cook for 10 minutes.

Crack eggs into the pan, season them with salt and pepper, cover pan and cook for 6 minutes more.

Sprinkle cilantro at the end and serve.

Enjoy!

Nutrition:

Calories: 46 kcal

Protein: 1.97 g

Fat: 0.49 g

Carbohydrates: 10.07 g

Sodium: 14 mg

2. Keto Breakfast Bowl.

Preparation time: 10 minutes

Cooking time: 20 minutes

Servings: 1

Ingredients

4 ounces beef, ground

1 avocado, pitted, peeled and chopped

1 yellow onion, chopped

8 mushrooms, sliced

2 eggs, whisked

12 black olives, pitted and sliced

1 tablespoon coconut oil

½ teaspoon smoked paprika

Salt and black pepper to the taste

Directions

Heat up a pan with the coconut oil over medium heat, add onions, mushrooms, salt and pepper, stir and cook for 5 minutes.

Add beef and paprika, stir, cook for 10 minutes and transfer to a bowl.

Heat up the pan again over medium heat, add eggs, some salt and pepper and scramble them.

Return beef mix to pan and stir.

Add avocado and olives, stir and cook for 1 minute.

Transfer to a bowl and serve. Enjoy!

Nutrition:

Calories: 423 kcal

Protein: 26.07 g

Fat: 29.87 g

Carbohydrates: 16.04 g

Sodium: 120 mg

3. Yummy Eggs and Sausages.

Preparation time: 10 minutes

Cooking time: 35 minutes

Servings: 6

Ingredients

5 tablespoons ghee

12 eggs

1-ounce spinach, torn

12 ham slices

2 sausages, chopped

1 yellow onion, chopped

1 red bell pepper, chopped

Salt and black pepper to the taste

Directions

Heat up a pan with 1 tablespoon ghee over medium heat, add sausages and onion, stir and cook for 5 minutes.

Add bell pepper, salt and pepper, stir and cook for 3 minutes more and transfer to a bowl.

Melt the rest of the ghee and divide into 12 cupcake molds.

Add a slice of ham in each cupcake mold, divide spinach in each and then the sausage mix.

Crack an egg on top, put everything in the oven and bake at 425 degrees F for 20 minutes.

Leave your Keto cupcakes to cool down a bit before serving.

Enjoy!

Nutrition:

Calories: 332 kcal

Protein: 26.27 g

Fat: 22.47 g

Carbohydrates: 5.16 g

Sodium: 799 mg

4. Breakfast Scrambled Eggs

Preparation time: 10 minutes

Cooking time: 10 minutes

Servings: 1

Ingredients

4 bell mushrooms, chopped

3 eggs, whisked

2 ham slices, chopped

¼ cup red bell pepper, chopped

½ cup spinach, chopped

1 tablespoon coconut oil

Salt and black pepper to the taste

Directions

Heat up a pan with half of the oil over medium heat, add mushrooms, spinach, ham and bell pepper, stir and cook for 4 minutes.

Heat up another pan with the rest of the oil over medium heat, add eggs and scramble them.

Add veggies and ham, salt and pepper, stir, cook for 1 minute and serve.

Enjoy!

Nutrition:

Calories: 594 kcal

Protein: 38.45 g

Fat: 44.5 g

Carbohydrates: 11.71 g

Sodium: 914 mg

5. Delicious Frittata

Preparation time: 10 minutes

Cooking time: 1 hour

Servings: 4

Ingredients

9 ounces spinach

12 eggs

1-ounce pepperoni

5 ounces mozzarella, shredded

½ cup parmesan, grated

½ cup ricotta cheese

1 teaspoon garlic, minced

4 tablespoons olive oil

A pinch of nutmeg

Salt and black pepper to the taste

Directions

Squeeze liquid from spinach and put in a bowl.

In another bowl, mix eggs with salt, pepper, nutmeg and garlic and whisk well.

Add spinach, parmesan and ricotta and whisk well again.

Pour this into a pan, sprinkle mozzarella and pepperoni on top, put in the oven and bake at 375 degrees F for 45 minutes.

Leave frittata to cool down for a few minutes before serving it.

Enjoy!

Nutrition:

Calories: 704 kcal

Protein: 49.35 g

Fat: 50.3 g

Carbohydrates: 12.84 g

Sodium: 888 mg

6. Smoked Salmon Breakfast.

Preparation time: 10 minutes

Cooking time: 10 minutes

Servings: 3

Ingredients

4 eggs, whisked

4 ounces smoked salmon, chopped

½ teaspoon avocado oil

For the sauce:

1 cup coconut milk

½ cup cashews, soaked, drained

¼ cup green onions, chopped

1 teaspoon garlic powder

1 tablespoon lemon juice

Salt and black pepper to the taste

Directions

In your blender, mix cashews with coconut milk, garlic powder and lemon juice and blend well.

Add salt, pepper and green onions, blend again well, transfer to a bowl and keep in the fridge for now.

Heat up a pan with the oil over medium-low heat, add eggs, whisk a bit and cook until they are almost done.

Put in your preheated broiler and cook until eggs set.

Divide eggs on plates, top with smoked salmon and serve with the green onion sauce on top.

Enjoy!

Nutrition:

Calories: 559 kcal

Protein: 28.03 g

Fat: 41.69 g

Carbohydrates: 21.03 g

Sodium: 463 mg

7. Feta and Asparagus Delight.

Preparation time: 10 minutes

Cooking time: 25 minutes

Servings: 2

Ingredients

12 asparagus spears

1 tablespoon olive oil

2 green onions, chopped

1 garlic clove, minced

6 eggs

Salt and black pepper to the taste

½ cup feta cheese

Directions

Heat up a pan with some water over medium heat, add asparagus, cook for 8 minutes, drain well, chop 2 spears and reserve the rest.

Heat up a pan with the oil over medium heat, add garlic, chopped asparagus and onions, stir and cook for 5 minutes.

Add eggs, salt and pepper, stir, cover and cook for 5 minutes.

Arrange the whole asparagus on top of your frittata, sprinkle cheese, put in the oven at 350 degrees F and bake for 9 minutes.

Divide between plates and serve.

Enjoy!

Nutrition:

Calories: 582 kcal

Protein: 33.93 g

Fat: 44.06 g

Carbohydrates: 12.09 g

Sodium: 664 mg

8. Special Breakfast Eggs

Preparation time: 10 minutes

Cooking time: 4 minutes

Servings: 12

Ingredients

4 tea bags - 4 tablespoons salt

12 eggs - 2 tablespoons cinnamon

6-star anise

1 teaspoon black pepper

1 tablespoon peppercorns

8 cups water

1 cup tamari sauce

Directions

Put water in a pot, add eggs, bring them to a boil over medium heat and cook until they are hard boiled.

Cool them down and crack them without peeling.

In a large pot, mix water with tea bags, salt, pepper, peppercorns, cinnamon, star anise and tamari sauce.

Add cracked eggs, cover pot, bring to a simmer over low heat and cook for 30 minutes.

Discard tea bags.

Leave eggs to cool down, peel and serve them for breakfast.

Enjoy!

Nutrition:

Calories: 146 kcal

Protein: 9.39 g

Fat: 10.39 g

Carbohydrates: 3.71 g

Sodium: 2596 mg

9. Eggs Baked In Avocados

Preparation time: 10 minutes

Cooking time: 20 minutes

Servings: 4

Ingredients

2 avocados, cut in halves and pitted

4 eggs

Salt and black pepper to the taste

1 tablespoon chives, chopped

Directions

Scoop some flesh from the avocado halves and arrange them in a baking dish.

Crack an egg in each avocado, season with salt and pepper, put them in the oven at 425 degrees F and bake for 20 minutes.

Sprinkle chives at the end and serve for breakfast!

Enjoy!

Nutrition:

Calories: 295 kcal

Protein: 11.23 g

Fat: 24.4 g

Carbohydrates: 10.68 g

Sodium: 110 mg

10. Shrimp and Bacon Breakfast.

Preparation time: 10 minutes

Cooking time: 15 minutes

Servings: 4

Ingredients

1 cup mushrooms, sliced

4 bacon slices, chopped

4 ounces smoked salmon, chopped

4 ounces shrimp, deveined

Salt and black pepper to the taste

½ cup coconut cream

Directions

Heat up a pan over medium heat, add bacon, stir and cook for 5 minutes.

Add mushrooms, stir and cook for 5 minutes more.

Add salmon, stir and cook for 3 minutes.

Add shrimp and cook for 2 minutes.

Add salt, pepper and coconut cream, stir, cook for 1 minute, take off heat and divide between plates.

Enjoy!

Nutrition:

Calories: 277 kcal

Protein: 16.17 g

Fat: 22.82 g

Carbohydrates: 3.32 g

Sodium: 281 mg

Chapter 15: Vegetables Recipes

11. Spinach Soup

Preparation time: 10 minutes

Cooking time: 15 minutes

Servings: 8

Ingredients

Butter – 2 tbsp.

Spinach – 20 ounces, chopped

Garlic – 1 tsp. minced

Salt and ground black pepper to taste

Chicken stock – 45 ounces

Ground nutmeg – ½ tsp.

Heavy cream – 2 cups

Onion – 1, chopped

Directions

Heat a saucepan and melt the butter.

Add the onion, and stir-fry for 4 minutes.

Add garlic, and stir-fry for 1 minute.

Add spinach and stock, and stir-fry for 5 minutes. Remove from heat.

Blend soup with a hand mixer and heat the soup again.

Add salt, pepper, nutmeg, cream, stir, and cook for 5 minutes.

Serve.

Nutrition:

Calories: 158

Fat: 14.7g

Carb: 5.4g

Protein: 3.3g

Sodium: 87 mg

12. Asparagus Frittata

Preparation time: 10 minutes

Cooking time: 15 minutes

Servings: 4

Ingredients

Onion – ¼ cup, chopped

A drizzle of olive oil

Asparagus spears – 1-pound, cut into 1-inch pieces

Salt and ground black pepper to taste

Eggs – 4, whisked

Cheddar cheese – 1 cup, grated

Directions:

Heat a pan with oil over medium heat.

Add onions, and stir-fry for 3 minutes.

Add asparagus and stir-fry for 6 minutes.

Add eggs and stir-fry for 3 minutes.

Add salt, pepper, and sprinkle with cheese.

Place in the oven and broil for 3 minutes.

Divide frittata on plates and serve.

Nutrition:

Calories: 202

Fat: 13.3g

Carb: 5.8g

Protein: 15.1g

Sodium: 106 mg

13. Bell Peppers Soup

Preparation time: 10 minutes

Cooking time: 15 minutes

Servings: 6

Ingredients

Roasted bell peppers – 12, seeded and chopped

Olive oil – 2 tbsp. - Garlic – 2 cloves, minced - Vegetable stock – 30 ounces

Salt and black pepper to taste - Water - 6 ounces

Heavy cream – 2/3 cup

Onion – 1, chopped

Parmesan cheese – ¼ cup, grated

Celery stalks – 2, chopped

Directions:

Heat a saucepan with oil over medium heat.

Add onion, garlic, celery, salt, and pepper. Stir-fry for 8 minutes.

Add water, bell peppers, stock, stir, and bring to a boil. Cover, lower heat, and simmer for 5 minutes.

Remove from heat and blend with a hand mixer.

Then adjust seasoning and add cream. Stir and bring to a boil.

Remove from the heat and serve on bowls.

Sprinkle with Parmesan and serve.

Nutrition:

Calories: 155

Fat: 12g

Carb: 8.6g

Protein: 4.7g

Sodium: 90 mg

14. Radish Hash Browns

Preparation time: 10 minutes

Cooking time: 10 minutes

Servings: 4

Ingredients

Onion powder – ½ tsp.

Radishes – 1 pound, shredded

Garlic powder – ½ tsp.

Salt and ground black pepper to taste

Eggs – 4

Parmesan cheese – 1/3 cup, grated

Directions:

In a bowl, mix radishes, with salt, pepper, onion, garlic powder, eggs, Parmesan cheese, and mix well.

Spread on a lined baking sheet.

Place in an oven at 375° F and bake for 10 minutes.

Serve and enjoy!

Nutrition:

Calories: 104

Fat: 6g

Carb: 4.5g

Protein: 8.6g

Sodium: 276 mg

15. Celery Soup

Preparation time: 10 minutes

Cooking time: 30 minutes

Servings: 6

Ingredients

Celery – 1 bunch, chopped

Onion – 1, chopped

Green onion – 1 bunch, chopped

Garlic cloves – 4, minced

Salt and ground black pepper to taste

Parsley – 1 fresh bunch, chopped

Fresh mint bunches – 2, chopped

Persian lemons – 3 dried, pricked with a fork

Water – 2 cups

Olive oil – 4 Tbsp.

Directions:

Heat a saucepan with oil over medium heat.

Add onion, garlic, and green onions. Stir and cook for 6 minutes.

Add Persian lemons, celery, salt, pepper, water, stir, cover pan, and simmer on medium heat for 20 minutes.

Add parsley and mint, stir, and cook for 10 minutes.

Blend with a hand mixer and serve.

Nutrition:

Calories: 100

Fat: 9.5g

Carb: 4.4g

Protein: 1g

Sodium: 55 mg

16. Spring Greens Soup

Preparation time: 10 minutes

Cooking time: 30 minutes

Servings: 4

Ingredients

Mustard greens – 2 cups, chopped

Collard greens – 2 cups, chopped

Vegetable stock – 4 cups

Onion – 1, chopped

Salt and ground black pepper to taste

Coconut aminos – 2 Tbsp.

Fresh ginger – 2 tsp. grated

Directions:

Put the stock into a saucepan and bring to a simmer over medium heat.

Add ginger, coconut aminos, salt, pepper, onion, mustard, and collard greens. Stir, cover, and cook for 30 minutes. Remove from the heat.

Blend the soup with a hand mixer.

Serve.

Nutrition:

Calories: 35

Fat: 1g

Carb: 7g

Protein: 2g

Sodium: 64 mg

17. Alfalfa Sprouts Salad

Preparation time: 10 minutes

Cooking time: 10 minutes

Servings: 4

Ingredients

Dark sesame oil – 1 ½ tsp.

Alfalfa sprouts – 4 cups

Salt and ground black pepper to taste

Grapeseed oil – 1 ½ tsp.

Coconut yogurt – ¼ cup

Directions:

In a bowl, mix sprouts with yogurt, grape seed oil, sesame oil, salt, and pepper. Toss to coat and serve.

Nutrition:

Calories: 83

Fat: 7.6g

Carb: 3.4g

Protein: 1.6g

Sodium: 19 mg

18. Eggplant Stew

Preparation time: 10 minutes

Cooking time: 30 minutes

Servings: 4

Ingredients

Onion – 1, chopped - Garlic – 2 cloves, chopped - Fresh parsley – 1 bunch, chopped

Salt and black pepper to taste

Dried oregano – 1 tsp.

Eggplants – 2, cut into chunks

Olive oil – 2 Tbsp.

Capers – 2 Tbsp. chopped

Green olives – 12, pitted and sliced

Tomatoes – 5, chopped

Herb vinegar – 3 Tbsp.

Directions:

In a saucepan, heat oil over medium heat.

Add oregano, eggplant, salt, pepper, and stir-fry for 5 minutes.

Add parsley, onion, garlic, and stir-fry for 4 minutes.

Add tomatoes, vinegar, olives, capers, and stir-fry for 15 minutes.

Adjust seasoning and stir.

Serve.

Nutrition:

Calories: 280

Fat: 17.9g

Carb: 8.4g

Protein: 5.4g

Sodium: 308 mg

19. Zucchini Salad

Preparation time: 10 minutes

Cooking time: 10 minutes

Servings 6

Ingredients:

2 pounds zucchini - 2 tbsp butter or olive oil - 3 oz celery stalks, finely sliced

2 oz chopped scallions - 1 cup mayonnaise - 2 pounds zucchini

2 tbsp butter or olive oil -- 3 oz celery stalks, finely sliced

2 oz chopped scallions - 1 cup mayonnaise

2 tbsp fresh chives, finely chopped

½ tablespoons Dijon Mustard

Sea Salt

Pepper

Directions:

Peel and cut the zucchini into pieces that are about half an inch thick. Use a spoon to remove the seeds. Place in a colander and add salt. Leave for 5 – 10 minutes and then cautiously press out the water.

Fry the cubes in butter for a couple of minutes over medium heat. They should not brown, just slightly soften. Set aside to cool.

Mix the other ingredients in a large bowl and add the zucchini once it's cool.

Tip: You can prepare the salad 1-2 days ahead of time; the flavors only enhance with time. You can also add a chopped hard- boiled egg.

Nutrition:

Calories 312

Protein 3g

Fat 32g

Carbs 4g

Sodium: 676 mg

20. Loaded Baked Cauliflower

Preparation time: 10 minutes

Cooking time: 30 minutes

Servings 2

Ingredients:

4 ounces bacon

1 pound cauliflower

2/3 cup sour cream

½ pound cheddar cheese, shredded

2 tbsp chives, finely chopped

1 tsp garlic powder

Sea salt

Freshly ground pepper

Directions:

Preheat oven to 350° F.

Chop the bacon into small pieces. Fry until crispy in a hot frying pan. Reserve the fat for serving.

Break the cauliflower into florets. Boil until soft in lightly salted water. Drain completely.

Chop the cauliflower roughly. Add sour cream and garlic powder. Combine well with ¾ of the cheese and most of the finely chopped chives. Salt and pepper

Place in a baking dish and top with the rest of the cheese. Bake in the oven for 10 – 15 minutes or until the cheese has melted.

Top with the bacon, the rest of the chives and the bacon fat. Enjoy!

Nutrition:

Calories 1014

Protein 40g

Fat 89g

Carbs 13g

Sodium: 2213 mg

Chapter 16: Fish and Seafood Recipes

21. Salmon Skewers

Preparation time: 35 mins

Cooking time: 30 mins

Servings: 4

Ingredients:

¼ c fresh spinach, chopped fine - 1 lb salmon cut into bite-sized pieces

¼ t black pepper, freshly ground - ½ t pink Himalayan salt - 1 T olive oil

3½ oz sliced prosciutto

1 c full-fat mayonnaise

8 wooden or metal skewers

Directions:

Heat oven to 400 degrees.

Mix olive oil spinach salt and pepper in a 1-gallon storage bag.

Coat salmon pieces in oil mixture by placing them in the bag.

Place salmon on skewers.

Wrap salmon skewers with prosciutto.

Bake salmon for approximately 15 minutes turning every 3 or 4 minutes.

When prosciutto is crispy, and salmon is cooked, remove from oven.

Serve with mayonnaise on the side.

Nutrition:

Calories: 680

Carbohydrates: 1g

Protein: 28g

Fat: 62g

Sodium: 1092 mg

22. Coconut Salmon with Napa Cabbage

Preparation time: 45 mins

Cooking time: 40 mins

Servings: 4

Ingredients: 1¼ lbs salmon - 1 T olive oil - ½ c unsweetened shredded coconut

1 t turmeric - 1 t kosher salt - ½ t garlic powder - 4 T olive oil, for frying

2 c Napa cabbage - 1 stick butter

Salt and pepper

Directions:

Cut salmon into small 1-inch chunks. Grind coconut to make it more likely to stay on the fish pieces. If you don't have a grinder, use a sharp knife to chop the shredded coconut as finely as possible. Mix coconut, turmeric, salt, and garlic powder in a bowl. In another bowl, coat salmon with 1 tablespoon of olive oil. Roll the oil-coated salmon in dry ingredients. Heat 4 tablespoons of olive oil in a frying pan to medium heat.

Cook coconut coated salmon until crispy. It will take about one minute per side. Make sure each side gets nicely browned. Remove cooked salmon from the pan and keep warm while cooking the cabbage Slice cabbage into thin strips with a knife or shred in a food processor. Melt butter in pan used to cook salmon. Cook cabbage until tender. Season cabbage with salt and pepper.

Serve cabbage with salmon and enjoy.

Nutrition:

Calories: 744

Carbohydrates: 3g

Protein: 32g

Fat: 67g

Sodium: 1457 mg

23. Keto Tuna Casserole

Preparation time: 45 mins

Cooking time: 40 mins

Servings: 4

Ingredients:4 T butter - 2 T olive oil - 1 medium onion, diced

1 green bell pepper, diced

5 celery stalks, diced - 2 c baby spinach chopped fine

2 large cans tuna in olive oil, drained - 1 c mayonnaise

1 ½ c freshly shredded Parmesan cheese

1 t red pepper flakes

Salt and pepper

Directions:

Preheat oven to 350 degrees.

Heat butter and olive oil in a large skillet.

Sauté onions, green bell pepper, celery, and spinach in butter/oil.

In a bowl, mix tuna, Parmesan cheese, mayonnaise, and red pepper flake until thoroughly combined.

Add sautéed vegetables to the tuna mixture and stir until everything is incorporated

Pour tuna mixture into a casserole dish for baking.

Bake in the oven for 30 minutes.

Remove casserole from the oven when golden brown on top and bubbly.

Nutrition:

Calories: 953

Carbohydrates: 5g

Protein: 43g

Fat: 83g

Sodium: 1376 mg

24. Baked Fish Fillets with Vegetables in Foil

Preparation time: 10 minutes

Cooking time: 40 minutes

Servings 3

Ingredients: 1 lb. cod (or any white fish) - 1 red bell pepper, sliced

6 cherry tomatoes, halved

1 leek (small size, only the white part, sliced)

¼ onion, sliced - ½ zucchini, sliced - 1 clove garlic, chopped

2 tbsp olives - 1 oz butter - 2 tbsp olive oil

½ lemon sliced to taste

Coriander leaves, to taste (optional)

Salt and pepper to taste

Directions:

Preheat oven to 400° F.

Slice the zucchini, leek, onion, bell pepper and lemon, cut tomatoes in half, chop the garlic.

Transfer all the vegetables to a baking sheet lined with foil.

Cut the fish into bite-sized pieces and add to the vegetables. Add salt and pepper, drizzle olive oil and add pieces of butter around evenly.

Fold the foil and make sure you seal the joints of the foil tightly.

Bake for 35 – 40 minutes.

Can be served with aioli or any other low carb sauce of your choice.

Nutrition:

Calories 339

Fat 19g

Protein 35g

Carbs 5g

Sodium: 569 mg

25. Fish & Chips

Preparation time: 15 minutes

Cooking time: 30 minutes

Servings 2

Ingredients:

For chips:- ½ tbsp olive oil - 1 medium zucchini - Salt and pepper to taste

For fish:- ¾ lb. cod (or any white fish) - Oil for frying - ½ cup almond flour - ¼ tsp onion powder

For Sauce:

2 tbsp dill pickle relish - ¼ tbsp curry powder - ½ cup mayonnaise - ½ tsp paprika powder

½ cup parmesan cheese, grated - 1 egg - Salt and pepper to taste

Directions:

For the sauce, simply combine all the sauce ingredients in a bowl. Mix well and then set aside. Line some parchment paper on a baking sheet and preheat oven to 400°F. Make thin zucchini rods, brush them with oil, and spread them on the baking sheet. Add a pinch of salt and pepper on top. Bake for about 30 minutes or wait until the zucchini turns golden brown. While baking the zucchini, crack the egg in a bowl and beat thoroughly. On a separate plate, combine the parmesan cheese, almond flour, and the remaining spices.

Slice the fish into 1 inch by 1-inch pieces. Roll them on the flour mixture. Dip in the beaten egg and sprinkle more flour to cover the pieces again.

Place a deep saucepan on the heat with about 340-360°F. Heat the oil for a while, then fry the fish for three minutes on each side. Remove from the heat when it becomes golden brown but make sure that the fish is cooked through.

Transfer to a serving plate and serve with the baked Zucchini fries and tartar sauce. You can also use any other Keto-friendly sauce of your choice.

Nutrition:

Calories 463

Fat 26.2 g

Protein 49g

Carbs 6g

Sodium: 1607 mg

26. Baked Salmon with Almonds and Cream Sauce

Preparation time: 10 minutes

Cooking time: 20 minutes

Servings 2

Ingredients: Almond Crumbs Creamy Sauce - 3 tbsp shaved almonds

2 tbsp almond milk (for thinning the sauce if necessary) - ½ cup cream cheese

Salt to taste

Fish

1 salmon fillet (about ½ lb.) - 1 tsp coconut oil - 1 tbsp lemon zest

1 tsp salt

White pepper to taste

Directions:

Prepare the salmon: cut the salmon in half. Mix the lemon zest, salt and pepper together and rub the mixture on the salmon. Let it cool in the refrigerator for 20 minutes so the seasonings will be absorbed. Meanwhile, preheat the oven to 300° F.

Heat some coconut oil on a nonstick baking dish. Fry the fish on both sides for a few minutes and make sure that the fish is sealed. Top with almond crumbs and bake in the oven for 10 to 15 minutes.

Take the dish out of the oven and transfer the fish to a separate plate. Set aside.

Place the baking dish on a fire and add the cream cheese. Combine the fish baking juices and the cheese for a more flavorful sauce.

Mix well until uniformed. If necessary, add some almond milk to the sauce.

Pour the sauce onto the fish. Best served hot.

Nutrition:

Calories 522

Fat 44g

Protein 28g

Carbs 2.4g

Sodium Na1432 mg

27. Shrimp and Sausage Bake

Preparation time: 15 minutes

Cooking time: 20 minutes

Servings 4

Ingredients:

2 tbsp olive oil

6 ounces chorizo sausage, diced

½ pound (16 to 20 count) shrimp, peeled and deveined

½ small sweet onion, chopped

1 tsp minced garlic - ¼ cup Herbed Chicken Stock

Pinch red pepper flakes

1 red bell pepper, chopped

Directions:

Place a large skillet over medium-high heat and add the olive oil.

Sauté the sausage until it is warmed through, about 6 minutes.

Add the shrimp and sauté until it is opaque and just cooked through, about 4 minutes.

Remove the sausage and shrimp to a bowl and set aside.

Add the red pepper, onion, and garlic to the skillet and sauté until tender, about 4 minutes.

Add the chicken stock to the skillet along with the cooked sausage and shrimp.

Bring the liquid to a simmer and simmer for 3 minutes.

Stir in the red pepper flake and serve.

Nutrition:

Calories 323

Fat 24g

Protein 20g

Carbs 6g

Sodium 898 mg

28. Herb Butter Scallops

Preparation time: 10 minutes

Cooking time: 10 minutes

Servings 4

Ingredients:

1 pound sea scallops, cleaned

Freshly ground black pepper

8 tbsp butter, divided

2 tsp minced garlic   Juice of 1 lemon

2 tsp chopped fresh basil

1 tsp chopped fresh thyme

Directions:

Pat the scallops dry with paper towels and season them lightly with pepper.

Place a large skillet over medium heat and add 2 tablespoons of butter.

Arrange the scallops in the skillet, evenly spaced but not too close together and sear each side until they are golden brown, about 2 ½ minutes per side.

Remove the scallops to a plate and set aside.

Add the remaining 6 tablespoons of butter to the skillet and sauté the garlic until translucent, about 3 minutes.

Stir in the lemon juice, basil and thyme and return the scallops to the skillet, turning to coat them in the sauce.

Serve immediately.

Nutrition:

Calories 306

Fat 24g

Protein 19g

Carbs 4g

Sodium 283 mg

29. Pan Seared Halibut with Citrus Butter Sauce

Preparation time: 10 minutes

Cooking time: 15 minutes

Servings 4

Ingredients:

4 (5 oz) halibut fillets, 1 inch thick - Sea salt

Freshly ground pepper - ¼ cup butter - 2 tbsp minced garlic

1 shallot, minced - 3 tablespoons dry white wine - 1 tbsp freshly squeezed orange juice

1 tbsp freshly squeezed lemon juice - 2 tsp chopped fresh parsley

2 tsp olive oil

Directions:

Pat the fish dry with paper towels and then lightly season the fillets with salt and pepper. Set aside on a paper towel-lined plate.

Pace a small saucepan over medium heat and melt the butter.

Sauté the garlic and shallot until tender, about 3 minutes.

Whisk in the white wine, lemon juice, and orange juice and bring the sauce to a simmer, cooking until it thickens slightly, about 2 minutes.

Remove the sauce from the heat and stir in the parsley; set aside.

Place a large skillet over medium-high heat and add the olive oil.

Panfry the fish until lightly browned and just cooked through, turning them over once, about 10 minutes in total.

Serve the fish immediately with a spoonful of sauce for each.

Nutrition:

Calories 319

Fat 26g

Protein 22g

Carbs 2g

Sodium 509 mg

30. Baked Coconut Haddock

Preparation time: 10 minutes

Cooking time: 12 minutes

Servings 4

Ingredients:

4 (5 oz) boneless haddock fillets

Sea salt

Freshly ground pepper

1 cup shredded unsweetened coconut

½ cup ground hazelnuts

2 tbsp coconut oil, melted

Directions:

Preheat the oven to 400° F. Line a baking sheet with parchment paper and set aside.

Pat the fillets dry with paper towels and lightly season the with salt and pepper.

Stir together the shredded coconut and hazelnut in a small bowl.

Dredge the fish fillets in the coconut mixture so that both sides of each piece are thickly coated.

Place the fish on the baking sheet and lightly brush both sides of each piece with the coconut oil.

Bake the haddock until the topping is golden and the fish flakes easily with a fork, about 12 minutes total.

Serve.

Nutrition:

Calories 299

Fat 24g

Protein 20g

Carbs 1g

Sodium 63 mg

Chapter 17: Red Meat Recipes

31. Classic Pork Tenderloin

Preparation time: 15 minutes

Cooking time: 35 minutes

Servings: 4

Ingredients: 8 bacon slices - 2 lb. pork tenderloin - 1 tsp. dried oregano, crushed

1 tsp. dried basil, crushed - 1 tbsp. garlic powder - 1 tsp. seasoned salt - 3 tbsp. butter

Directions:

Preheat the oven to 400 degrees F. Heat a large ovenproof skillet over medium-high heat and cook the bacon for about 6-7 minutes. Transfer the bacon onto a paper towel lined plate to drain.

Then, wrap the pork tenderloin with bacon slices and secure with toothpicks.

With a sharp knife, slice the tenderloin between each bacon slice to make a medallion.

In a bowl, mix together the dried herbs, garlic powder and seasoned salt.

Now, coat the medallion with herb mixture.

With a paper towel, wipe out the skillet.

In the same skillet, melt the butter over medium-high heat and cook the pork medallion for about 4 minutes per side.

Now, transfer the skillet into the oven.

Roast for about 17-20 minutes.

Remove the wok from oven and let it cool slightly before cutting.

Cut the tenderloin into desired size slices and serve.

Nutrition:

Calories: 471

Carbohydrates: 1g

Protein: 53.5g

Fat: 26.6g

Sugar: 0.1g

Sodium: 1100mg

Fiber: 0.2g

32. Signature Italian Pork Dish

Preparation time: 15 minutes

Cooking time: 15 minutes

Servings: 6

Ingredients:

2 lb. pork tenderloins, cut into 1½-inch pieces - ¼ C. almond flour

1 tsp. garlic salt - Freshly ground black pepper, to taste

2 tbsp. butter

½ C. homemade chicken broth - 1/3 C. balsamic vinegar

1 tbsp. capers

2 tsp. fresh lemon zest, grated finely

Directions:

In a large bowl, add the pork pieces, flour, garlic salt and black pepper and toss to coat well.

Remove pork pieces from bowl and shake off excess flour mixture.

In a large skillet, melt the butter over medium-high heat and cook the pork pieces for about 2-3 minutes per side.

Add broth and vinegar and bring to a gentle boil.

Reduce the heat to medium and simmer for about 3-4 minutes.

With a slotted spoon, transfer the pork pieces onto a plate.

In the same skillet, add the capers and lemon zest and simmer for about 3-5 minutes or until desired thickness of sauce.

Pour sauce over pork pieces and serve.

Nutrition:

Calories: 373

Carbohydrates: 1.8g

Protein: 46.7g

Fat: 18.6g

Sugar: 0.4g

Sodium: 231mg

Fiber: 0.7g

33. Flavor Packed Pork Loin

Preparation time: 15 minutes

Cooking time: 1 hour

Servings: 6

Ingredients: 1/3 C. low-sodium soy sauce - ¼ C. fresh lemon juice

2 tsp. fresh lemon zest, grated - 1 tbsp. fresh thyme, finely chopped

2 tbsp. fresh ginger, grated - 2 garlic cloves, chopped finely

2 tbsp. Erythritol

Freshly ground black pepper, to taste

½ tsp. cayenne pepper - 2 lb. boneless pork loin

Directions:

For pork marinade: in a large baking dish, add all the ingredients except pork loin and mix until well combined.

Add the pork loin and coat with the marinade generously.

Refrigerate for about 24 hours.

Preheat the oven to 400 degrees F.

Remove the pork loin from marinade and arrange into a baking dish.

Cover the baking dish and bake for about 1 hour.

Remove from the oven and place the pork loin onto a cutting board.

With a piece of foil, cover each loin for at least 10 minutes before slicing.

With a sharp knife, cut the pork loin into desired size slices and serve.

Nutrition:

Calories: 230

Carbohydrates: 3.2g

Protein: 40.8g

Fat: 5.6g

Sugar: 1.2g

Sodium: 871mg

Fiber: 0.6g

34. Spiced Pork Tenderloin

Preparation time: 15 minutes

Cooking time: 18 minutes

Servings: 6

Ingredients:

2 tsp. fresh rosemary, minced - 2 tsp. fennel seeds - 2 tsp. coriander seeds - 2 tsp. caraway seeds

1 tsp. cumin seeds - 1 bay leaf

Salt and freshly ground black pepper, to taste

2 tbsp. fresh dill, chopped - 2 (1-lb.) pork tenderloins, trimmed

Directions:

For spice rub: in a spice grinder, add the seeds and bay leaf and grind until finely powdered. Add the salt and black pepper and mix. In a small bowl, reserve 2 tbsp. of spice rub. In another small bowl, mix together the remaining spice rub, and dill. Place 1 tenderloin over a piece of plastic wrap. With a sharp knife, slice through the meat to within ½-inch of the opposite side. Now, open the tenderloin like a book. Cover with another plastic wrap and with a meat pounder, gently pound into ½-inch thickness. Repeat with the remaining tenderloin. Remove the plastic wrap and spread half of the dill mixture over the center of each tenderloin. Roll each tenderloin like a cylinder. With a kitchen string, tightly tie each roll at several places. Rub each roll with the reserved spice rub generously. With 1 plastic wrap, wrap each roll and refrigerate for at least 4-6 hours. Preheat the grill to medium-high heat. Grease the grill grate. Remove the plastic wrap from tenderloins. Place tenderloins on the grill and cook for about 14-18 minutes, flipping occasionally.

Remove from the grill and place tenderloins onto a cutting board and with a piece of foil, cover each tenderloin for at least 5-10 minutes before slicing. With a sharp knife, cut the tenderloins into desired size slices and serve.

Nutrition:

Calories: 313

Carbohydrates: 1.4g

Protein: 45.7g

Fat: 12.6g

Sugar: 0g

Sodium: 127mg

Fiber: 0.7g

35. Sticky Pork Ribs

Preparation time: 15 minutes

Cooking time: 2 hours 34 minutes

Servings: 9

Ingredients:

¼ C. Erythritol - 1 tbsp. garlic powder - 1 tbsp. paprika - ½ tsp. red chili powder

4 lb. pork ribs, membrane removed - Salt and freshly ground black pepper, to taste

1½ tsp. liquid smoke - 1½ C. sugar-free BBQ sauce

Directions:

Preheat the oven to 300° degrees F. Line a large baking sheet with 2 layers of foil, shiny side out. In a bowl, add the Erythritol, garlic powder, paprika and chili powder and mix well. Season the ribs with salt and black pepper and then, coat with the liquid smoke. Now, rub the ribs with the Erythritol mixture.

Arrange the ribs onto the prepared baking sheet, meaty side down.

Arrange 2 layers of foil on top of ribs and then, roll and crimp edges tightly. Bake for about 2-2½ hours or until desired doneness. Remove the baking sheet from oven and place the ribs onto a cutting board.

Now, set the oven to broiler. With a sharp knife, cut the ribs into serving sized portions and evenly coat with the barbecue sauce.

Arrange the ribs onto a broiler pan, bony side up.

Broil for about 1-2 minutes per side.

Remove from the oven and serve hot.

Nutrition:

Calories: 530

Carbohydrates: 2.8g

Protein: 60.4g

Fat: 40.3g

Sugar: 0.4g

Sodium: 306mg

Fiber: 0.5g

36. Valentine's Day Dinner

Preparation time: 15 minutes

Cooking time: 35 minutes

Servings: 4

Ingredients: 1 tbsp. olive oil - 4 large boneless rib pork chops - 1 tsp. salt

1 C. cremini mushrooms, chopped roughly - 3 tbsp. yellow onion, chopped finely

2 tbsp. fresh rosemary, chopped - 1/3 C. homemade chicken broth - 1 tbsp. Dijon mustard

1 tbsp. unsalted butter - 2/3 C. heavy cream - 2 tbsp. sour cream

Directions:

Heat the oil in a large skillet over medium heat and sear the chops with the salt for about 3-4 minutes or until browned completely.

With a slotted spoon, transfer the pork chops onto a plate and set aside.

In the same skillet, add the mushrooms, onion and rosemary and sauté for about 3 minutes.

Stir in the cooked chops, broth and bring to a boil.

Reduce the heat to low and cook, covered for about 20 minutes.

With a slotted spoon, transfer the pork chops onto a plate and set aside.

In the skillet, stir in the butter until melted.

Add the heavy cream and sour cream and stir until smooth.

Stir in the cooked pork chops and cook for about 2-3 minutes or until heated completely.

Serve hot.

Nutrition:

Calories: 400

Carbohydrates: 3.6g

Protein: 46.3g

Fat: 21.6g

Sugar: 0.8g

Sodium: 820mg

Fiber: 1.1g

37. South East Asian Steak Platter

Preparation time: 15 minutes

Cooking time: 20 minutes

Servings: 4

Ingredients: 14 oz. grass-fed sirloin steak, trimmed and cut into thin strips

Freshly ground black pepper, to taste - 2 tbsp. olive oil, divided - 1 small yellow onion, chopped

2 garlic cloves, minced - 1 Serrano pepper, seeded and chopped finely

3 C. broccoli florets - 3 tbsp. low-sodium soy sauce - 2 tbsp. fresh lime juice

Directions:

Season steak with black pepper.

In a large skillet, heat 1 tbsp. of the oil over medium heat and cook the steak for about 6-8 minutes or until browned from all sides.

Transfer the steak onto a plate.

In the same skillet, heat the remaining oil and sauté onion for about 3-4 minutes.

Add the garlic and Serrano pepper and sauté for about 1 minute.

Add broccoli and stir fry for about 2-3 minutes.

Stir in cooked beef, soy sauce and lime juice and cook for about 3-4 minutes.

Serve hot.

Nutrition:

Calories: 282

Carbohydrates: 7.6g

Protein: 33.1g

Fat: 13.5g

Sugar: 2.7g

Sodium: 749mg

Fiber: 2.3g

38. Pesto Flavored Steak

Preparation time: 15 minutes

Cooking time: 17 minutes

Servings: 4

Ingredients:

¼ C. fresh oregano, chopped

1½ tbsp. garlic, minced

1 tbsp. fresh lemon peel, grated

½ tsp. red pepper flakes, crushed

Salt and freshly ground black pepper, to taste

1 lb. (1-inch thick) grass-fed boneless beef top sirloin steak

1 C. pesto

¼ C. feta cheese, crumbled

Directions:

Preheat the gas grill to medium heat. Lightly, grease the grill grate.

In a bowl, add the oregano, garlic, lemon peel, red pepper flakes, salt and black pepper and mix well.

Rub the garlic mixture onto the steak evenly.

Place the steak on the grill and cook, covered for about 12-17 minutes, flipping occasionally.

Remove from the grill and place the steak onto a cutting board for about 5 minutes.

With a sharp knife, cut the steak into desired sized slices.

Divide the steak slices and pesto onto serving plates and serve with the topping of the feta cheese.

Nutrition:

Calories: 226

Carbohydrates: 6.8g

Protein: 40.5g

Fat: 7.6g Sugar: 0.7g

Sodium: 579mg

Fiber: 2.2g

39. Flawless Grilled Steak

Preparation time: 21 minutes

Cooking time: 10 minutes

Servings: 5

Ingredients:

½ tsp. dried thyme, crushed - ½ tsp. dried oregano, crushed - 1 tsp. red chili powder

½ tsp. ground cumin - ¼ tsp. garlic powder

Salt and freshly ground black pepper, to taste

1½ lb. grass-fed flank steak, trimmed

¼ C. Monterrey Jack cheese, crumbled

Directions:

In a large bowl, add the dried herbs and spices and mix well.

Add the steaks and rub with mixture generously.

Set aside for about 15-20 minutes.

Preheat the grill to medium heat. Grease the grill grate.

Place the steak on the grill over medium coals and cook for about 17-21 minutes, flipping once halfway through.

Remove the steak from grill and place onto a cutting board for about 10 minutes before slicing.

With a sharp knife, cut the steak into desired sized slices.

Top with the cheese and serve.

Nutrition:

Calories: 271

Carbohydrates: 0.7g

Protein: 38.3g

Fat: 11.8g

Sugar: 0.1g

Sodium: 119mg

Fiber: 0.3g

40. Mongolian Beef

Preparation time: 15 minutes

Cooking time: 10 minutes

Servings: 4

Ingredients: 1 lb. grass-fed flank steak, cut into thin slices against the grain

2 tsp. arrowroot starch - Salt, to taste - ¼ C. avocado oil

1 (1-inch) piece fresh ginger, grated - 4 garlic cloves, minced - ½ tsp. red pepper flakes, crushed

¼ C. water - 1/3 C. low-sodium soy sauce - 1 tsp. red boat fish sauce

3 scallions, sliced - 1 tsp. sesame seeds

Directions:

In a bowl, add the steak slices, arrowroot starch and salt and toss to coat well.

In a larger skillet, heat oil over medium-high heat and cook the steak slices for about 1½ minutes per side.

With a slotted spoon, transfer the steak slices onto a plate.

Drain the oil from the skillet but leaving about 1 tbsp. inside.

In the same skillet, add the ginger, garlic and red pepper flakes and sauté for about 1 minute.

Add the water, soy sauce and fish sauce and stir to combine well.

Stir in the cooked steak slices and simmer for about 3 minutes.

Stir in the scallions and simmer for about 2 minutes.

Remove from the heat and serve hot with the garnishing of sesame seeds.

Nutrition:

Calories: 266

Carbohydrates: 5.7g

Protein: 34g

Fat: 11.7g

Sugar: 1.7g

Sodium: 1350mg

Fiber: 1.2g

Chapter 18: Bread Recipes

41. Holiday Morning Bread

Preparation time: 15 minutes

Cooking time: 50 minutes

Servings: 10

Ingredients:

1/3 C. unsweetened almond milk - ¼ C. granulated Erythritol - 2 tbsp. ground flax seeds

1 tsp. organic vanilla extract - ¾ C. homemade pumpkin puree - ½ C. coconut oil, softened

¾ C. organic soy flour - ¼ C. coconut flour - ½ tsp. organic baking powder - ¼ tsp. baking soda

1 tsp. ground cinnamon - ½ tsp. ground ginger - ½ tsp. ground cardamom - ¼ tsp. salt

Directions:

Preheat the oven to 350° F. Line a 9x5-inch loaf pan with parchment paper. In a bowl, add the almond milk, Erythritol, flax seeds and vanilla extract and mix until well combined. Set aside for about 5 minutes. Meanwhile, in another bowl, add the flours, baking powder, baking soda, spices and salt and mix until well combined. In the bowl of almond milk, add the pumpkin puree and coconut oil and beat until well combined.

Add the flour mixture and mix until well combined and smooth.

Place the mixture into the prepared loaf pan evenly.

Bake for about 50 minutes or until a toothpick inserted in the center comes out clean.

Remove the bread pan from oven and place onto a wire rack to cool for about 10 minutes.

Carefully, invert the bread onto the wire rack to cool completely before slicing.

With a sharp knife, cut the bread loaf into the desired sized slices and serve.

Nutrition:

Calories: 150

Carbohydrates: 6.8g

Protein: 4.2g

Fat: 12.5g

Sugar: 2.2g

Sodium: 106mg

Fiber: 3g

42. Masterpiece Bread

Preparation time: 15 minutes

Cooking time: 45 minutes

Servings: 12

Ingredients:

8 large organic eggs, room temperature

¾ C. coconut flour - 1/3 C. butter, melted - 1 tsp. organic baking powder

1 tsp. organic vanilla extract

¼ tsp. salt

1/3 C. fresh raspberries

Directions:

Preheat the oven to 350° F. Line a 9x5-inch loaf pan with parchment paper.

In a food processor, add the eggs and pulse on high speed until frothy and smooth.

Add the remaining ingredients except raspberries and pulse on high speed until smooth.

Place the mixture into the prepared loaf pan evenly.

Place the raspberries on top and gently, submerge into the dough.

Bake for about 40-45 minutes or until a toothpick inserted in the center comes out clean.

Remove the bread pan from oven and place onto a wire rack to cool for about 10 minutes.

Carefully, invert the bread onto the wire rack to cool completely before slicing.

With a sharp knife, cut the bread loaf into the desired sized slices and serve.

Nutrition:

Calories: 103

Carbohydrates: 1.9g

Protein: 4.4g

Fat: 8.6g

Sugar: 0.6g

Sodium: 233mg

Fiber: 0.6g

43. Dense Morning Bread

Preparation time: 15 minutes

Cooking time: 1 hour 10 minutes

Servings: 16

Ingredients:

2 C. blanched almond flour - 2 tsp. organic baking powder - ¼ tsp. salt

¾ C. Erythritol - ½ C. butter, softened - 3 large organic eggs

1 tbsp. fresh lemon juice - 1 tbsp. fresh lemon zest, grated - 1 tsp. organic vanilla extract

1½ C. zucchini, grated and squeezed - 1 C. fresh blueberries

Directions:

Preheat the oven to 325° F. Line a 9x5-inch loaf pan with parchment paper.

In a bowl, mix together the almond flour, baking powder and salt.

In another large bowl, add the Erythritol and butter and beat until fluffy.

Add the eggs, lemon juice, lemon zest and vanilla extract and beat until well combined. Add the flour mixture and beat until well combined.

Fold in the zucchini and blueberries.

Place the mixture into the prepared loaf pan evenly.

Bake for about 60-70 minutes or until a toothpick inserted in the center comes out clean.

Remove the bread pan from oven and place onto a wire rack to cool for about 10 minutes.

Carefully, invert the bread onto the wire rack to cool completely before slicing.

With a sharp knife, cut the bread loaf into the desired sized slices and serve.

Nutrition:

Calories: 153

Carbohydrates: 5.2g

Protein: 4.5g

Fat: 13.7g

Sugar: 1.7g

Sodium: 87mg

Fiber: 1.9g

44. Multi Seeds Bread

Preparation time: 1 minutes

Cooking time: 1 hour

Servings: 16

Ingredients:

1½ C. raw pumpkin seeds, divided - 1 C. raw sunflower seeds - ½ C. chia seeds

½ C. flax seeds - ½ C. psyllium husks - 1 tsp. pink Himalayan salt

1/8 tsp. powder stevia - 3 C. warm water - 3 tbsp. olive oil

Directions:

Preheat the oven to 350° F. Line a loaf pan with parchment paper. In a food processor, add 1 C. of pumpkin seeds and pulse until finely ground. In a large bowl, add the ground pumpkin seed, remaining whole pumpkin seeds, sunflower seeds, chia seeds, flax seeds, psyllium husks, salt and stevia and mix well. Add the warm water and oil and mix until well combined. Place the mixture into the prepared bread loaf pan evenly and with your hands, press to smooth the top surface. Bake for about 45 minutes. Carefully with the help of the parchment paper, remove the bread loaf from loaf pan. Arrange the loaf onto a baking sheet, top side down.

Bake for about 15 minutes or until a toothpick inserted in the center comes out clean.

Remove the baking sheet from oven and place onto a wire rack to cool for about 15 minutes.

Carefully, invert the bread onto the wire rack to cool completely before slicing.

With a sharp knife, cut the bread loaf into the desired sized slices and serve.

Nutrition:

Calories: 151

Carbohydrates: 7.9g

Protein: 5.2g

Fat: 12.4g

Sugar: 0.3g

Sodium: 153mg

Fiber: 5.2g

45. Sandwich Bread

Preparation time: 15 minutes

Cooking time: 45 minutes

Servings: 16

Ingredients:

2 C. almond flour - 1 tsp. organic baking powder - ½ tsp. xanthan gum

½ tsp. salt - 7 large organic eggs - ½ C. butter, melted

2 tbsp. coconut oil

Directions:

Preheat the oven to 350° F. Line an 8-inch loaf pan with parchment paper.

In a bowl, mix together the almond flour, baking powder, xanthan gum and salt.

In another large bowl, add the eggs and with an electric mixer, beat on high for about 1-2 minutes.

Add the melted butter and coconut oil and beat until smooth.

Add the flour mixture and beat until well combined.

Place the mixture into the prepared loaf pan evenly.

Bake for about 45 minutes or until a toothpick inserted in the center comes out clean.

Remove the bread pan from oven and place onto a wire rack to cool for about 10 minutes.

Carefully, invert the bread onto the wire rack to cool completely before slicing.

With a sharp knife, cut the bread loaf into the desired sized slices and serve.

Nutrition:

Calories: 178

Carbohydrates: 4.4g

Protein: 5.8g

at: 16.6g

Sugar: 0.7g

Sodium: 148mg

Fiber: 1.6g

46. Magic Cheese Bread

Preparation time: 15 minutes

Cooking time: 17 minutes

Servings: 6

Ingredients:

½ C. almond flour - 1 tbsp. Erythritol - 1 tbsp. organic baking powder

2 tsp. active dry yeast - 2½ C. mozzarella cheese, shredded

2 tbsp. cream cheese, softened - 2 large organic eggs, beaten

Directions:

Preheat oven to 400° F. Line a loaf pan with parchment paper.

In a bowl, mx together the almond flour, Erythritol, yeast and baking powder.

In a microwave-safe bowl, add the mozzarella cheese and cream cheese and microwave for about 1-2 minutes or until melted completely, stirring after every 30 seconds.

Add the flour mixture and mix until well combined.

Add the eggs and mix until a dough ball forms

Place the mixture into the prepared loaf pan evenly.

Bake for about 12-15 minutes or until a toothpick inserted in the center comes out clean.

Remove the bread pan from oven and place onto a wire rack to cool for about 10 minutes.

Carefully, invert the bread onto the wire rack to cool completely before slicing.

With a sharp knife, cut the bread loaf into the desired sized slices and serve.

Nutrition:

Calories: 128

Carbohydrates: 4.3g

Protein: 8.1g

Fat: 9.6g

Sugar: 0.5g

Sodium: 107mg

Fiber: 1.3g

47. 10-Minutes Bread

Preparation time: 10 minutes

Cooking time: 10 minutes

Servings: 1

Ingredients:

3 tbsp. almond flour

1 tbsp. butter, melted

½ tsp. organic baking powder

1 large organic egg

Pinch of salt

Directions:

Preheat oven to 375° F. Lightly, grease an oven safe container.

In a bowl, add all ingredients and mix until well combined.

Place the mixture into the prepared container evenly.

Bake for about 10 minutes or until a toothpick inserted in the center comes out clean.

Remove the bread pan from oven and place onto a wire rack to cool for about 10 minutes.

Carefully, invert the bread onto the wire rack to cool completely before serving.

Nutrition:

Calories: 296

Carbohydrates: 9g

Protein: 10.9g

Fat: 6.1g

Sugar: 1.1g

Sodium: 309mg

Fiber: 2.3g

48. Subtle Rosemary Bread

Preparation time: 15 minutes

Cooking time: 50 minutes

Servings: 10

Ingredients:

½ C. coconut flour - 1 tsp. organic baking powder - 2 tsp. dried rosemary - ½ tsp. onion powder

½ tsp. garlic powder - ¼ tsp. salt - 6 large organic eggs - ½ C. butter, melted

Directions:

Preheat oven to 350° F. Grease an 8x4 loaf pan

In a bowl, mix together the coconut flour, baking powder, rosemary, spices and salt.

In another bowl, add the eggs and with a hand mixer, beat until bubbly.

Slowly, add the butter and beat until smooth.

Slowly, add the flour mixture and beat until well combined.

Place the mixture into the prepared bread loaf pan evenly.

Bake for about 40-50 minutes or until a toothpick inserted in the center comes out clean.

Remove the loaf pan from oven and place onto a wire rack to cool for about 10 minutes.

Carefully, invert the bread onto the wire rack.

With a sharp knife, cut the bread loaf into the desired sized slices and serve warm.

Nutrition:

Calories: 130

Carbohydrates: 1.2g

Protein: 4g

Fat: 12.3g

Sugar: 0.4g

Sodium: 168mg

Fiber: 0.4g

49. Brunch Time Bread

Preparation time: 15 minutes

Cooking time: 1 hour

Servings: 10

Ingredients: 7 oz. bacon, chopped - 1½ C. almond flour - 1 tbsp. organic baking powder

2 organic eggs - 1/3 C. sour cream - 4 tbsp. butter, melted and cooled - 1 C. cheddar cheese, shredded

Directions:

Preheat the oven to 300° F. Line a loaf pan with greased parchment paper.

Heat a nonstick frying pan over medium heat and cook the bacon for about 8-10 minutes or until crispy.

With a slotted spoon, transfer the bacon onto a plate to drain.

In a bowl, mix together the almond flour and baking powder.

In another bowl, add the eggs and sour cream and beat until smooth.

Add the flour mixture and mix until well combined.

Add the melted butter and mix well.

Gently, fold in the cooked bacon and cheese.

Place the mixture into the prepared bread loaf pan evenly.

Bake for about 45-50 minutes or until a toothpick inserted in the center comes out clean.

Remove the loaf pan from oven and place onto a wire rack to cool for about 10 minutes.

Carefully, invert the bread onto the wire rack.

With a sharp knife, cut the bread loaf into the desired sized slices and serve warm.

Nutrition:

Calories: 321

Carbohydrates: 5.1g

Protein: 15.2g

Fat: 27.6g

Sugar: 0.7g

Sodium: 583mg

Fiber: 1.8g

50. Amazing Cheddar Bread

Preparation time: 15 minutes

Cooking time: 45 minutes

Servings: 10

Ingredients:

2 C. almond flour - 1 tsp. baking powder - ½ tsp. xanthan gum - ½ tsp. salt

6 organic eggs - ½ C. butter, softened - 1½ C. cheddar cheese, shredded and divided

2 tbsp. garlic powder - 1 tbsp. parsley flakes - ½ tbsp. dried oregano

Directions:

Preheat oven to 350° F. Line a loaf pan with parchment paper.

In a bowl, mix together the flour, baking powder, xanthan gum and salt.

In another bowl, add the eggs and beat until frothy

Add the butter and mix well.

Slowly, add the flour mixture and mix well.

Add 1 C. of cheese, garlic powder, parsley and oregano and mix well.

Place the mixture into the prepared bread loaf pan evenly and top with the remaining cheese.

Bake for about 45 minutes or until a toothpick inserted in the center comes out clean.

Remove the loaf pan from oven and place onto a wire rack to cool for about 10 minutes.

Carefully, invert the bread onto the wire rack.

With a sharp knife, cut the bread loaf into the desired sized slices and serve warm.

Nutrition:

Calories: 323

Carbohydrates: 7g

Protein: 12.8g

Fat: 28.7g

Sugar: 1.5g

Sodium: 328mg

Fiber: 2.9g

Chapter 19: Salad Recipes

51. Keto Cobb Salad

Preparation time: 15 minutes

Cooking time: 5 minutes

Servings: 1

Ingredients:

4 cherry tomatoes, diced

1 avocado, sliced

1 hardboiled egg, sliced

2 oz. chicken breast, shredded

1 oz. feta cheese, crumbled

¼ cup cooked bacon, crumbled

2 cups mixed green salad

Directions:

Mix the green salad in a large bowl. Add the chicken breast, feta cheese, and the crumbled bacon.

Put the tomatoes, avocado, egg, chicken, bacon, and feta cheese on top of the greens.

Enjoy! You can also try adding some ranch dressing but be aware that this adds to the total fat and calorie content of your salad.

Nutrition:

Calories 412

Fat 23.6g

Cholesterol 264.3mg

Fiber 6g

Protein 38.4g

52.   5 Ingredient Keto Salad

Preparation time: 20 minutes

Cooking time: 10 to 15 minutes

Servings: 2

Ingredients:

2 boneless chicken breasts with skin - 1 large avocado, sliced - 3 slices of bacon

4 cups mixed leafy greens of choice - 2 tbsp. dairy-free ranch dressing

Salt and pepper to taste

Duck fat for greasing

Directions:

Start by preheating the oven to 200 degrees Celsius or 400 degrees Fahrenheit.

Season the chicken with salt and pepper. Grab a skillet and grease it with duck fat before cooking the chicken on the hot pan.

Keep the heat on high until you get a golden-brown skin surface. This should take around 5 minutes per side.

Once done, you can cook the chicken in the oven for 10 to 15 minutes. You can also put the bacon in with the chicken to save on the cooking time. You can also fry it in a pan, depending your personal preferences.

After cooking, let the chicken rest for a few minutes.

Slice the avocado and the cooked chicken. Start assembling your salad, adding together the leafy greens, crispy bacon, sliced chicken, and avocado. Use 2 tablespoons of ranch dressing. Mix together until all ingredients are thoroughly coated. Enjoy!

Nutrition:

Carbs 3.1g

Protein 38.7g

Fat 43.8g

Calories 581

53. Vegetarian Keto Cobb

Preparation time: 10 minutes

Cooking time: 0 minutes

Servings: 3

Ingredients:

3 large hard boiled eggs, sliced - 4 ounces cheddar cheese, cubed - 2 tbsp. sour cream

2 tbsp. mayonnaise - ½ tsp. garlic powder - ½ tsp. onion powder

1 tsp. dried parsley - 1 tbsp. milk - 1 tbsp. Dijon mustard

3 cups romaine lettuce, torn - 1 cup cucumber, diced

½ cup cherry tomatoes, halved

Directions:

The dressing is a combination of the sour cream, mayonnaise, and dried herbs. Mix them well together until full combined.

Add one tablespoon of milk into the mix until you get the thickness you want.

Layer in the salad, adding all the ingredients that's not part of the dressing recipe. Put the mustard on the center of the salad.

Drizzle with your dressing and enjoy! Each serving should have just 2 tablespoons of dressing to meet the nutritional information given below.

Nutrition:

Calories 330

Fat 26.32g

Protein 16.82g

Net carbohydrates 4.83g

54. Keto Chicken Salad w/ Avocado

Preparation time: 25 minutes

Cooking time: 20 minutes

Servings: 2

Ingredients: 2 pcs. of boneless chicken thigh fillets - 2 tbsp. olive oil - ¼ cup water

1 tsp. salt - 1 tsp. sweet chili powder - 1 tsp. dried thyme - ½ tsp. ground black pepper

4 cloves garlic - Handful of cherry tomatoes (salad) - 2 cups arugula (salad)

1 cup purslane leaves (salad) - ½ cup fresh dill (salad)

1 tbsp. olives (salad) - 1 tsp. sesame seeds (salad) - 1 tsp. nigella seeds (salad)

½ tbsp. olive oil (salad)

2 tbsp. avocado dressing (salad)

1 avocado, sliced (salad)

Basil leaves (salad)

Directions:

Pour ¼ cup of water on a skillet and cook the chicken fillets over medium heat, keeping the lid covered until the water drains completely.

Drizzle 2 tbsp. of olive oil on the chicken. Add some garlic cloves and then season it with salt and pepper. Add some thyme and sweet chili powder. Cook them again until golden, making sure you flip the chicken every now and again to even out the sides.

Put all the salad ingredients in a bowl. Put in some nigella seeds and sesame seeds with some olive oil and avocado dressing. Mix and enjoy!

Nutrition:

Calories 1093

Sugar 17g

Fat 81g

Protein 68g

Carbohydrates 34g.

55. Keto Chicken Salad

Preparation time: 30 minutes

Cooking time: 20 to 25 minutes

Servings: 4

Ingredients:

2 cups cooked chicken, shredded

2 boiled eggs, chopped

¼ cup pecans, chopped

¼ cup dill pickles, chopped

½ cup mayonnaise

¼ cup minced yellow onion

1 tsp. yellow mustard

1 tsp. white distilled vinegar

1 tsp. fresh dill

Salt and pepper to taste

Directions:

Except for the chicken, add everything together in a mixing bowl and stir together until thoroughly combined.

Add the chicken and stir well, making sure that all of the chicken are well coated.

Add salt and pepper to taste.

Chill in the fridge for one hour before serving. You can keep it stored in the fridge for 3 to 5 days.

Nutrition:

Calories 394

Saturated fat 33g

Trans fat 6g

Cholesterol 25g

Carbohydrates 3g

Sugar 1g

Protein 21g

56. Tuna Fish Salad – Quick and Easy!

Preparation time: 15 minutes

Cooking time: 10 minutes maximum

Servings: 1

Ingredients:

10 kalamata olives, pitted 1 small zucchini sliced lengthwise

½ diced avocado 2 cups of mixed greens 1 large diced tomato

1 sliced green onion

1 can chunk light tuna in water, drained ¼ cup fresh parsley, chopped

½ cup fresh mint, chopped

1 tbsp. extra virgin olive oil

1 tbsp. balsamic vinegar

¼ tsp. fine sea salt

¾ tsp. black pepper, cracked

Directions:

Grill the zucchini slices on both sides for a few minutes or as desired. Once cooked, cut it into bite-size pieces.

Grab a large bowl and just put all the ingredients together in the container, mixing them together until the liquid ingredients are evenly distributed.

Serve while still fresh. This salad would taste best if eaten immediately so try not to have any leftovers.

Nutrition:

Calories 563

Total fat 30.9g

Carbohydrates 37.5g

Dietary fiber 15.7g

Protein 41.8g

57. Potluck Lamb Salad

Preparation time: 20 minutes

Cooking time: 10 minutes

Servings: 4

Ingredients: 2 tbsp. olive oil, divided

12 oz. grass-fed lamb leg steaks, trimmed

Salt and freshly ground black pepper, to taste

6½ oz. halloumi cheese, cut into thick slices

2 jarred roasted red bell peppers, sliced thinly

2 cucumbers, cut into thin ribbons

3 C. fresh baby spinach

2 tbsp. balsamic vinegar

Directions:

In a skillet, heat 1 tbsp. of the oil over medium-high heat and cook the lamb steaks for about 4-5 minutes per side or until desired.

Transfer the lamb steaks onto a cutting board for about 5 minutes.

Then cut the lamb steaks into thin slices.

In the same skillet, add halloumi and cook for about 1-2 minutes per side or until golden.

In a salad bowl, add the lamb, haloumi, bell pepper, cucumber, salad leaves, vinegar and remaining oil and toss to combine.

Serve immediately.

Nutrition:

Calories: 420

Carbohydrates: 8g

Protein: 35.4g

Fat: 27.2g

Sugar: 4g

Sodium: 417mg

Fiber: 1.3g

58. Spring Supper Salad

Preparation time: 15 minutes

Cooking time: 5 minutes

Servings: 5

Ingredients:

For Salad: 1 lb. fresh asparagus, trimmed and cut into 1-inch pieces

½ lb. smoked salmon, cut into bite-sized pieces

2 heads red leaf lettuce, torn   ¼ C. pecans, toasted and chopped

For Dressing: ¼ C. olive oil

2 tbsp. fresh lemon juice

1 tsp. Dijon mustard

Salt and freshly ground black pepper, to taste

Directions:

In a pan of boiling water, add the asparagus and cook for about 5 minutes.

Drain the asparagus well.

In a serving bowl, add the asparagus and remaining salad ingredients and mix.

In another bowl, add all the dressing ingredients and beat until well combined.

Place the dressing over salad and gently, toss to coat well.

Serve immediately.

Nutrition:

Calories: 223

 Carbohydrates: 8.5g

Protein: 11.7g

Fat: 17.2g

Sugar: 3.4g

Sodium: 960mg

Fiber: 3.5g

59. Chicken-of-Sea Salad

Preparation time: 15 minutes

Cooking time: 0 minutes

Servings: 6

Ingredients:

2 (6-oz.) cans olive oil packed tuna, drained

2 (6-oz.) cans water packed tuna, drained

¾ C. mayonnaise

2 celery stalks, chopped

¼ of onion, chopped

1 tbsp. fresh lime juice

2 tbsp. mustard

Freshly ground black pepper, to taste

6 C. fresh baby arugula

Directions:

In a large bowl, add all the ingredients except arugula and gently stir to combine.

Divide arugula onto serving plates and top with tuna mixture.

Serve immediately.

Nutrition:

Calories: 325

Carbohydrates: 2.7g

Protein: 27.4g

Fat: 22.2g

Sugar: 0.9g

Sodium: 389mg

Fiber: 1.1g

60. Yummy Roasted Cauliflower

Preparation time: 15 minutes

Cooking time: 20 minutes

Servings: 5

Ingredients:

4 C. cauliflower florets

4 small garlic cloves, peeled and halved

2 tbsp. olive oil

1 tbsp. fresh lemon juice

1 tsp. dried thyme, crushed

1 tsp. dried oregano, crushed

½ tsp. red pepper flakes, crushed

Salt and freshly ground black pepper, to taste

Directions:

Preheat the oven to 425 degrees F. Generously, grease 2 large baking dishes.

In a large bowl, add all the ingredients and toss to coat well.

Divide the cauliflower mixture into the prepared baking dishes evenly and spread in a single layer.

Roast for about 15-20 minutes or until the desired doneness, tossing 2 times.

Remove from the oven and serve hot.

Nutrition:

Calories: 74

Carbohydrates: 5.5g

Protein: 1.8g

Fat: 5.8g

Sugar: 2gS

odium: 56mg

Fiber: 2.3g

Chapter 20: Snack Recipes

61. Marinated Eggs.

Preparation time: 2 hours and 10 minutes

Cooking time: 7 minutes

Servings: 4

Ingredients:

6 eggs 1 and ¼ cups water

¼ cup unsweetened rice vinegar 2 tablespoons coconut aminos

Salt and black pepper to the taste 2 garlic cloves, minced

1 teaspoon stevia 4 ounces cream cheese

1 tablespoon chives, chopped

Directions

Put the eggs in a pot, add water to cover, bring to a boil over medium heat, cover and cook for 7 minutes.

Rinse eggs with cold water and leave them aside to cool down.

In a bowl, mix 1 cup water with coconut aminos, vinegar, stevia and garlic and whisk well.

Put the eggs in this mix, cover with a kitchen towel and leave them aside for 2 hours rotating from time to time.

Peel eggs, cut in halves and put egg yolks in a bowl.

Add ¼ cup water, cream cheese, salt, pepper, and chives and stir well.

Stuff egg whites with this mix and serve them.

Enjoy!

Nutrition:

Calories: 289 kcal

Protein: 15.86 g

Fat: 22.62 g

Carbohydrates: 4.52 g

Sodium: 288 mg

62. Sausage and Cheese Dip.

Preparation time: 10 minutes

Cooking time: 2 hours and 10 minutes

Servings: 28

Ingredients:

8 ounces cream cheese

A pinch of salt and black pepper

16 ounces sour cream

8 ounces pepper jack cheese, chopped

15 ounces canned tomatoes mixed with habaneros

1 pound Italian sausage, ground

¼ cup green onions, chopped

Directions

Heat up a pan over medium heat, add sausage, stir and cook until it browns.

Add tomatoes mix, stir and cook for 4 minutes more.

Add a pinch of salt, pepper and the green onions, stir and cook for 4 minutes.

Spread pepper jack cheese on the bottom of your slow cooker.

Add cream cheese, sausage mix and sour cream, cover and cook on High for 2 hours.

Uncover your slow cooker, stir dip, transfer to a bowl and serve.

Enjoy!

Nutrition:

Calories: 132 kcal

Protein: 6.79 g

Fat: 9.58 g

Carbohydrates: 6.22 g

Sodium: 362 mg

63. Tasty Onion and Cauliflower Dip.

Preparation time: 2 hours 10 minutes

Cooking time: 30 minutes

Servings: 24

Ingredients:

1 and ½ cups chicken stock

1 cauliflower head, florets separated

¼ cup mayonnaise

½ cup yellow onion, chopped

¾ cup cream cheese

½ teaspoon chili powder

½ teaspoon cumin, ground

½ teaspoon garlic powder

Salt and black pepper to the taste

Directions

Put the stock in a pot, add cauliflower and onion, heat up over medium heat and cook for 30 minutes.

Add chili powder, salt, pepper, cumin and garlic powder and stir.

Also add cream cheese and stir a bit until it melts.

Blend using an immersion blender and mix with the mayo.

Transfer to a bowl and keep in the fridge for 2 hours before you serve it.

Enjoy!

Nutrition:

Calories: 40 kcal

Protein: 1.23 g

Fat: 3.31 g

Carbohydrates: 1.66 g

Sodium: 72 mg

64. Pesto Crackers.

Preparation time: 10 minutes

Cooking time: 17 minutes

Servings: 6

Ingredients:

½ teaspoon baking powder

Salt and black pepper to the taste

1 and ¼ cups almond flour ¼ teaspoon basil, dried 1 garlic clove, minced

2 tablespoons basil pesto

A pinch of cayenne pepper

3 tablespoons ghee

Directions

In a bowl, mix salt, pepper, baking powder and almond flour.

Add garlic, cayenne and basil and stir.

Add pesto and whisk.

Also add ghee and mix your dough with your finger.

Spread this dough on a lined baking sheet, introduce in the oven at 325 degrees F and bake for 17 minutes.

Leave aside to cool down, cut your crackers and serve them as a snack.

Enjoy!

Nutrition:

Calories: 9 kcal

Protein: 0.41 g

Fat: 0.14 g

Carbohydrates: 1.86 g

Sodium: 2 mg

65. Pumpkin Muffins.

Preparation time: 10 minutes

Cooking time: 15 minutes

Servings: 18

Ingredients:

¼ cup sunflower seed butter

¾ cup pumpkin puree 2 tablespoons flaxseed meal ¼ cup coconut flour

½ cup erythritol ½ teaspoon nutmeg, ground

1 teaspoon cinnamon, ground ½ teaspoon baking soda 1 egg ½ teaspoon baking powder

A pinch of salt

Directions

In a bowl, mix butter with pumpkin puree and egg and blend well.

Add flaxseed meal, coconut flour, erythritol, baking soda, baking powder, nutmeg, cinnamon and a pinch of salt and stir well.

Spoon this into a greased muffin pan, introduce in the oven at 350 degrees F and bake for 15 minutes.

Leave muffins to cool down and serve them as a snack.

Enjoy!

Nutrition:

Calories: 65 kcal

Protein: 2.82 g

Fat: 5.42 g

Carbohydrates: 2.27 g

Sodium: 57 mg

66. Taco Flavored Cheddar Crisps

Preparation time: 20 mins

Cooking time: 15 mins

Servings: 6

Ingredients:

¾ c sharp cheddar cheese, finely shredded

¼ c parmesan cheese, finely shredded

¼ t chili powder

¼ t ground cumin

Directions:

Preheat the oven to 400 degrees.

Line cookie sheet with parchment paper.

In a bowl, toss all ingredients together until well mixed.

Make 12 piles of cheese parchment paper.

Press down the cheese into a thin layer of cheese.

Bake for 5 minutes until cheese is bubby.

Allow to cool on parchment paper.

When completely cool, peel the paper away from the crisps.

These are a good Keto substitute for chips. They are cheesy and crisp. Enjoy!

Nutrition:

Calories: 13 kcal

Protein: 1.36 g

Fat: 0.2 g

Carbohydrates: 1.43 g

Sodium: 42 mg

67. Keto Seed Crispy Crackers

Preparation time: 1 hour

Cooking time: 55 mins

Servings: 30

Ingredients: ⅓ cup almond flour - ⅓ cup sunflower seed kernels - ⅓ cup pumpkin seed kernels

⅓ cup flaxseed - ⅓ cup chia seeds - 1 tbsp ground psyllium husk powder

1 tsp salt -¼ cup melted coconut oil

1 cup boiling water

Directions:

Preheat the oven to 300 degrees.

Stir all dry ingredients together in a medium-sized bowl until thoroughly mixed.

Add coconut oil and boiling water to dry ingredients and stir until all ingredients are well mixed.

On a flat surface, roll the dough between two pieces of parchment paper until approximately ⅛ inch thick.

Slide the dough, still between parchment paper onto a baking sheet.

Remove the top layer of parchment paper and place dough on a baking sheet into the oven.

Bake 40 minutes until golden brown.

Score the top of the dough into cracker sized pieces.

Leave in the oven to cool down.

When the big cracker is cool, break into pieces.

These crackers can be stored in an airtight container after they are completely cool.

Nutrition:

Calories: 61

Carbohydrates: 1g

Protein: .2g

Fat: .6g

Sodium: 90 mg

68. Parmesan Crackers

Preparation time: 10 minutes

Cooking time: 5 minutes

Servings: 8

Ingredients:

Butter – 1 tsp.

Full-fat parmesan – 8 ounces, shredded

Directions

Preheat the oven to 400° F.

Line a baking sheet with parchment paper and lightly grease the paper with the butter.

Spoon the parmesan cheese onto the baking sheet in mounds, spread evenly apart.

Spread out the mounds with the back of a spoon until they are flat.

Bake about 5 minutes, or until the center are still pale, and edges are browned.

Remove, cool, and serve.

Nutrition:

Calories: 133

Fat: 11g

Carb: 1g

Protein: 11g

Sodium: 483 mg

69. Deviled Eggs

Preparation time: 15 minutes

Cooking time: 10 minutes

Servings: 12

Ingredients:

Large eggs – 6, hardboiled, peeled, and halved lengthwise

Creamy mayonnaise – ¼ cup

Avocado – ¼, chopped

Swiss cheese – ¼ cup, shredded

Dijon mustard – ½ tsp.

Ground black pepper

Bacon slices – 6, cooked and chopped

Directions

Remove the yolks and place them in a bowl. Place the whites on a plate, hollow-side up.

Mash the yolks with a fork and add Dijon mustard, cheese, avocado, and mayonnaise. Mix well and season yolk mixture with the black pepper.

Spoon the yolk mixture back into the egg white hollows and top each egg half with the chopped bacon.

Serve.

Nutrition:

Calories: 85

Fat: 7g

Carb: 2g

Protein: 6g

Sodium: 108 mg

70. Almond Garlic Crackers

Preparation time: 10 minutes

Cooking time: 15 minutes

Servings: 4

Ingredients:

Almond flour – ½ cup

Ground flaxseed – ½ cup

Shredded Parmesan cheese – 1/3 cup

Garlic powder – 1 tsp.

Salt – ½ tsp.

Water as needed

Directions

Line a baking sheet with parchment paper and preheat the oven to 400° F.

In a bowl, mix salt, Parmesan cheese, garlic powder, water, ground flaxseed, and almond meal. Set aside for 3 to 5 minutes.

Put dough on the baking sheet and cover with plastic wrap. Flatten the dough with a rolling pin.

Remove the plastic wrap and score the dough with a knife to make dents.

Bake in the oven for 15 minutes.

Remove, cool, and break into individual crackers.

Nutrition:

Calories: 96

Fat: 14g

Carb: 4g

Protein: 4g

Sodium: 446 mg

Chapter 21: Smoothies Recipes

71. Coconut Green Smoothie

Preparation time: 5 mins

Cooking time: 0 mins

Servings: 1

Ingredients:

⅔ c slightly defrosted frozen chopped spinach

½ avocado

1 T coconut oil

½ t matcha powder

1 T monk fruit sweetener

½ c coconut milk (from the dairy section, not canned)

⅔ c water

½ cup of ice

Directions:

Add all ingredients except the ice into a blender. Blend until everything is blended well.

Pulse in the ice until it is evenly distributed.

Pour into a glass.

This smoothie is good for fiber and fat. You can add flaxseed or softened chia seeds to the smoothie for additional fiber and nutrients. Fresh spinach can be used and may be substituted with fresh or frozen kale.

Nutrition:

Calories: 341

Carbohydrates: 3.9g

Protein: 5.6g

Fat: 24.7g

Sodium: 146 mg

72. Strawberry Smoothie

Preparation time: 5 mins

Cooking time: 0 mins

Servings: 1

Ingredients:

¼ c heavy cream

¾ c unsweetened vanilla almond milk

2 t stevia

½ c frozen strawberries (whole or sliced)

½ c ice (preferably crushed)

Directions:

Blend ingredients in a blender until blended well.

Pour into a tall glass.

Serve.

Nutrition:

Calories: 302

Carbohydrates: 8g

Protein: 2g

Fat: 26g

Sodium: 158 mg

73. Keto Mojito

Preparation time: 4 mins

Cooking time: 0 mins

Servings: 1

Ingredients

4 fresh mint leaves

2 T fresh lime Juice

2 t stevia

Ice

1.5 oz shot of white rum

Splash club soda or plain seltzer

Fresh mint as garnish

Instructions:

Muddle the mint, lime juice, and stevia for 10 seconds in the glass in which the drink will be served.

Fill the glass with ice, either cubed or crushed.

Pour the shot of rum over the ice.

Add club soda to fill the glass

Garnish with a mint leaf.

You may want to strain the drink after muddling to remove the broken mint leaves, so they don't get in the way of enjoying the drink. You can substitute the rum with vodka.

Nutrition:

Calories: 109

Carbohydrates: 2g

Protein: 0.16 g

Fat: 0.02 g

Sodium: 102 mg

74. Diabetic Friendly Smoothie

Preparation time: 10 minutes

Cooking time: 0 minutes

Servings: 2

Ingredients:

2 C. fresh baby spinach

½ avocado, peeled, pitted and chopped

1 tbsp. raw hemp seeds, shelled

4-6 drops liquid stevia

½ tsp. ground cinnamon

2 C. chilled alkaline water

Directions:

In a high-speed blender, add all the ingredients and pulse until smooth.

Transfer into 2 serving glasses and serve immediately.

Nutrition:

Calories: 137

Carbohydrates: 5.7g

Protein: 3.1g

Fat: 12.2g

Sugar: 0.3g

Sodium: 15mg

Fiber: 4.3g

75. Super Green Smoothie

Preparation time: 10 minutes

Cooking time: 0 minutes

Servings: 2

Ingredients:

2 tsp. green spirulina powder

1½ C. fresh spinach

1 C. cucumber, chopped

1 tbsp. chia seeds

1½ C. unsweetened almond milk

¼ C. ice cubes

Directions:

In a high-speed blender, add all the ingredients and pulse until smooth.

Transfer into 2 serving glasses and serve immediately.

Nutrition:

Calories: 64

Carbohydrates: 6.3g

Protein: 3.8g

Fat: 4.2g

Sugar: 1g

Sodium: 178mg

Fiber: 2g

76. Overpowering Smoothie

Preparation time: 10 minutes

Cooking time: 0 minutes

Servings: 2

Ingredients:

½ avocado, peeled, pitted and chopped

2 C. fresh spinach

1 scoop collagen protein powder

1 tbsp. sunflower seed butter

1 tsp. organic vanilla extract

½ tbsp. MCT oil

8-10 drops liquid stevia

1 C. unsweetened almond milk

1 C. ice cubes

Directions:

In a high-speed blender, add all the ingredients and pulse until smooth.

Transfer into 2 serving glasses and serve immediately.

Nutrition:

Calories: 261

Carbohydrates: 8.9g

Protein: 1.4g

Fat: 17.6g

Sugar: 0.7g

Sodium: 132mg

Fiber: 4.5g

77. Garden Fresh Smoothie

Preparation time: 10 minutes

Cooking time: 0 minutes

Servings: 2

Ingredients:

1 small zucchini, peeled and sliced

¾ C. fresh spinach, chopped

1 tsp. ground cinnamon

2 tbsp. Swerve

1½ C. unsweetened almond milk

½ C. ice cubes

Directions:

In a high-speed blender, add all the ingredients and pulse until smooth.

Transfer into 2 serving glasses and serve immediately.

Nutrition:

Calories: 50

Carbohydrates: 6.8g

Protein: 1.4g

Fat: 1.8g

Sugar: 1.1g

Sodium: 152mg

Fiber: 2.3g

78. Anti-Oxidant Smoothie

Preparation time: 10 minutes

Cooking time: 0 minutes

Servings: 2

Ingredients:

1 tsp. green matcha powder

1 tbsp. hot water

½ of medium avocado, peeled, pitted and chopped

2 tbsp. unflavored collagen powder

2 tbsp. Swerve

½ tsp. organic vanilla extract

¼ C. heavy whipping cream

1¼ C. unsweetened almond milk

¼ C. ice cubes

Directions:

In a small bowl, add the matcha powder and hot water and beat until well combined.

In a high-speed blender, add the matcha powder mixture and remaining ingredients and pulse until smooth.

Transfer into 2 serving glasses and serve immediately.

Nutrition:

Calories: 228

Carbohydrates: 7.1g

Protein: 12.9g

Fat: 17.5g

Sugar: 0.4g

Sodium: 133mg

Fiber: 4g

79. Coffee Smoothie

Preparation time: 5 Minutes

Cooking time: 5 Minutes

Servings: 1

Ingredients:

5 oz. cold coffee

3 oz. heavy cream

3 oz. almond milk

1 oz. sugar free chocolate syrup

1 oz. caramel syrup

1 tablespoon cocoa

12 oz. ice

Directions

In a blender place all the ingredients and blend until smooth.

Pour in a glass and serve.

Nutrition:

Calories: 2006 kcal

Protein: 34.68 g

Fat: 156.63 g

Carbohydrates: 129.9 g

Sodium: 382 mg

80. Chai Pumpkin Smoothie

Preparation time: 5 Minutes

Cooking time: 5 Minutes

Servings: 1

Ingredients:

¾ cup coconut milk

2 tablespoon pumpkin puree

1 tablespoon MCT oil

1 tsp chai tea

1 tsp alcohol free vanilla

½ tsp pumpkin pie spice

½ frozen avocado

Directions

In a blender place all the ingredients and blend until smooth.

Pour in a glass and serve.

Nutrition:

Calories: 793 kcal

Protein: 10.6 g

Fat: 78.62 g

Carbohydrates: 21.46 g

Sodium: 73 mg

Chapter 22: Soup and Stew Recipes

81. Chicken and Riced Cauliflower Soup

Preparation time: 45 mins

Cooking time: 40 mins

Servings: 4

Ingredients: 2 T olive oil 2 stalks celery with tops, chopped ¼ c onions, chopped

Salt and pepper, to taste 2 cloves garlic, minced ½ t paprika

4 c unsalted organic chicken bone broth 2 c chicken thigh meat, cut into 1/2" cubes

2 c diced cauliflower

Directions:

Heat the oil in a large saucepan over medium heat.

Add celery and onions and season with salt and pepper. Cook, stirring frequently, until vegetables are tender, about 5 minutes.

Add garlic and paprika. If needed, add another tablespoon of olive oil to the pan with the garlic, so the garlic cooks evenly. Sauté and cook until garlic is soft. This will take a minute or so.

Stir in chicken bone broth and bring to a boil.

Add chicken and diced cauliflower and simmer the soup until the chicken is cooked and the cauliflower is tender, but not overcooked.

Season with additional salt and pepper to taste.

Serve hot.

Nutrition:

Calories: 196

Carbohydrates: 4.8g

Protein: 26.4g

Fat: 10.4g

Sodium: 1147 mg

82. Spicy Creamy Chicken Soup

Preparation time: 4 hrs 30 mins

Cooking time: 4 hrs 20 mins

Servings: 4

Ingredients: 1 lb chicken breasts on the bone 1 c onion, diced 4 cloves garlic, minced

1 jalapeño pepper, chopped 1 T cumin ½ T chili powder

1 t salt 3 T lime juice

2 c low sodium organic chicken broth 1 8 oz package of cream cheese

½ c cilantro, chopped

Directions:

Add the chicken, onion, garlic, jalapeño, cumin, chili powder, paprika, salt, lime juice, and chicken broth to a slow cooker.

Cook in the slow cooker, covered, for 4 hours on the lowest setting.

After chicken is cooked through, remove from the pot and let cool until it can be easily handled.

Pull the chicken off the bone and shred or chop into bite-sized pieces.

Add the cream cheese to hot soup. Stir slowly until melted.

Add shredded chicken into the pot and stir to mix.

Bring the soup back up to temperature and turn off the heat.

Spoon into bowls and sprinkle cilantro on top.

Serve immediately.

Add a sprinkle of cheddar to add cheesy flavor to the soup.

Nutrition:

Calories: 424

Carbohydrates: 6g

Protein: 41g

Fat: 25g

Sodium: 2070 mg

83. Broccoli Cheese Soup

Preparation time: 50 mins

Cooking time: 45 mins

Servings: 6

Ingredients:

4 c broccoli florets

4 cloves minced garlic

3 ½ c low sodium vegetable broth

1 c heavy cream

3 c shredded sharp cheddar cheese

Directions:

In a large pot, sauté garlic in butter, ghee, or olive oil for one minute over medium heat.

Add vegetable broth, heavy cream, and chopped broccoli.

Heat soup to boiling, then reduce heat and simmer for 10-20 minutes, until broccoli is tender.

Use an immersion blender to puree the broccoli in the soup. If you do not have an immersion blender, use a slotted spoon to remove the broccoli and blend in a blender or food processor. After the broccoli is pureed, stir it back into the soup pot.

Reduce the heat under the soup and slowly add the cheddar into the soup, stirring frequently until melted.

Puree the soup again with the stick blender or regular blender.

Remove the soup from heat and serve in bowls.

Nutrition:

Calories: 291

Carbohydrates: 4g

Protein: 13g

Fat: 25g

Sodium: 98 mg

84. Low Carb Vegetarian Ramen

Preparation time: 35 minutes

Cooking time: 30 minutes

Servings: 4

Ingredients: 4 cups filtered water 4 pastured eggs 1 tbsp sugar-free red curry paste

1 tbsp coconut oil 2 tsp ground ginger 1 tsp ground turmeric 1 tsp garlic powder

2 cups full-fat canned coconut milk 1 cup of purple cabbage, chopped

1 cup of large-sized shredded rainbow carrots 1 cup Brussels sprouts, halved

2 large zucchinis, spiralized Salt and pepper to taste

Directions:

Grab a large pot and pour the water inside it, bringing it to a boil.

When boiling, add the coconut milk and spices. Reduce the heat to medium-low. Put in the cabbage, Brussels sprouts, and carrots. Stir in a while before adding the curry paste and coconut oil. Cook until the vegetables are soft and tender. This should take about 20 minutes While waiting, soft boil the eggs. This should take about 6 minutes. Take it out of the pot and put in cold water. When the vegetables are soft, put in the zucchini and allow it to cook for 4 minutes.

Your vegetarian ramen is ready. Serve it with the peeled and halved eggs.

Put in some lime juice and cilantro.

Nutrition:

Calories 237

Fat 15g

Total carbohydrates 15g

Fiber 4g

Sugar 7g

Protein 10g.

Sodium 159 mg

85. Low Carb Smoked Salmon Chowder

Preparation time: 25 minutes

Cooking time: 20 minutes

Servings: 6

Ingredients:

1 stalk celery chopped   1 clove garlic minced   2 tbsp salted butter

2 tbsp capers   2 tbsp chopped red onion   1 tbsp tomato paste

½ tsp salt ¼ cup chopped onion 1½ cups chicken broth

1½ cups heavy whipping cream   4 oz cream cheese   6 oz smoked salmon hot smoked, chopped

Directions:

Grab a large saucepan and melt butter in it using medium heat.

Put onion, celery, and sprinkle some salt onto the pan.

Sauté until the vegetables are tender.

Put in the onion until fragrant.

Add the chicken broth and tomato paste.

Allow the mix to simmer, constantly stirring until you get a smooth concoction.

In the meantime, put the cream cheese in a blender and put some of the broth mixture inside it. Blend until smooth. You can do this slowly if this will make it easier.

Put the broth back in the saucepan and add the salmon, capers, and cream.

Allow it to simmer again for a few minutes. The soup is ready now. Before serving, try sprinkling some chopped red onion on top.

Nutrition:

Calories 373

Carbohydrates 31.84g

Fiber 0.5g

Protein 12.9g

Sodium 750 mg

86. Keto Broccoli Soup

Preparation time: 10 Minutes

Cooking time: 30 Minutes

Servings: 4

Ingredients

Olive oil

1 cup chicken broth

1 cup heavy whipping cream

6 oz. Shredded cheddar cheese

Salt

5-ounces broccoli

1 celery stalk

1 small carrot

½ onion

Directions

In a pot add olive oil over medium heat.

Add onion, carrot, celery and cook for 2-3 minutes.

Add chicken broth and simmer for 4-5 minutes.

Stir in broccoli and cream.

Sprinkle in cheese and season with salt.

Nutrition:

Calories: 292 kcal

Protein: 20.7 g

Fat: 19.25 g

Carbohydrates: 9.47 g

Sodium: 751 mg

87. Keto Taco Soup

Preparation time: 10 Minutes

Cooking time: 10 Minutes

Servings: 8

Ingredients

2 lbs. ground beef

1 onion

1 cup heavy whipping cream

1 tsp chili powder

14 oz. cream cheese

1 tsp garlic

1 tsp cumin

2 10 oz. cans tomatoes

16 oz. beef broth

Directions

Cook for a couple of minutes, onion, garlic and beef.

Add cream cheese and stir until fully melted.

Add tomatoes, whipping cream, beef broth, stir and bring to boil.

Serve.

Nutrition:

Calories: 535 kcal

Protein: 46.48 g

Fat: 35.86 g

Carbohydrates: 6.3 g

Sodium: 432 mg

88. Keto Chicken Soup

Preparation time: 10 Minutes

Cooking time: 30 Minutes

Servings: 4

Ingredients

2 boneless chicken breasts

20-ounces diced tomatoes

½ tsp salt

1 cup salsa

6-ounces cream cheese

Avocado

2 tablespoons taco seasoning

1 cup chicken broth

Directions

In a slow cooker place all ingredients and cook for 5-6 hours or until chicken is tender.

Whisk cream cheese into the broth.

When ready, remove and serve.

Nutrition:

Calories: 605 kcal

Protein: 50.06 g

Fat: 37.47 g

Carbohydrates: 17.59 g

Sodium: 1644 mg

89. Keto Spinach Soup

Preparation time: 5 Minutes

Cooking time: 15 Minutes

Servings: 2

Ingredients

¼ lbs. spinach

2 oz. onion

¼ lbs. heavy cream

½ oz. garlic

1 chicken stock cube

1,5 cup water

1 tablespoons butter

Directions

In a saucepan melt the butter and sauté the onion.

Add garlic, spinach and stock cube and half the water.

Cook until spinach wilts.

Pour everything in a blender and blend, add water.

Serve with pepper and toasted nuts.

Nutrition:

Calories: 286 kcal

Protein: 3.96 g

Fat: 27.13 g

Carbohydrates: 9.2 g

Sodium: 415 mg

90. Keto Toscana Soup

Preparation time: 10 Minutes

Cooking time: 30 Minutes

Servings: 4

Ingredients

1 lb. Italian sausage

½ cup whipping cream

1 tsp garlic

2 cup kale leaves

1 bag radishes 16-ounces

1 onion

30-ounces vegetable broth

Directions

Cut radishes into small chunks and blend until smooth.

In a pot add onion and sausage, cook until brown, add radishes, broth.

Cook on medium heat, add heavy whipping cream, kale leaves.

Cook for a couple minutes.

Remove and serve.

Nutrition:

Calories: 2175 kcal

Protein: 22.45 g

Fat: 235.07 g

Carbohydrates: 19.06 g

Sodium: 1030 mg

Chapter 23: Dessert Recipes

91.   Chocolate Mug Muffin

Preparation time: 2 minutes

Cooking time: 2 minutes

Servings 2

Ingredients:

2 tbsp almond flour   1 tbsp cocoa powder 1 tbsp Swerve

½ tsp baking powder ¼ tsp vanilla extract

1 egg

1 pinch sea salt

1 ½ tbsp melted coconut oil or butter

½ ounce sugar-free dark chocolate

½ tsp coconut oil or butter for greasing the mugs

Directions:

Combine dry ingredients in a small bowl. Stir in egg and melted coconut oil or butter. Mix until smooth.

Add coarsely chopped chocolate and pour into two well-greased coffee mugs.

Microwave for 90 seconds. Remove and let cool

Serve with a spoonful of whipped coconut cream.

Nutrition:

Calories 230

Protein 6g

Fat 21g

Carbs 2g

Sodium 160mg

92. Almond Cookies

Preparation time: 10 minutes

Cooking time: 20 minutes

Servings: 18

Ingredients

Almond butter – 2 tbsp.   Coconut oil – 1 tbsp.   Coconut milk – ¼ cup

Sugar-free coconut syrup – 2 tbsp.   Eggs – 2 large   Baking powder – ½ tsp.

Salt – ½ tsp.

Granulated sugar substitute – 2 tbsp.   Sugar-free dried coconut – 1 ½ cup

Flax meal – ½ cup   90% dark chocolate – 2 squares

Almond – 18

Directions

In a bowl, combine the coconut oil and almond butter and mix well.

Add the eggs, syrup, and coconut milk and mix until smooth.

Stir in the flax meal, dried coconut, sweetener, salt, and baking powder.

Roll the dough into 18 (1-inch) balls and place on a parchment covered cookie sheet.

Press lightly to make a dent on each ball.

Top with chopped chocolate (each cookie) and top with an almond.

Bake in a preheated 375° F/190° C oven until browned and slightly puffed, about 20 minutes.

Serve.

Nutrition:

Calories 114

Fat 11g

Carb 4g

Protein 3g

Sodium 88 mg

93. Pumpkin Pie Cupcakes

Preparation time: 15 minutes

Cooking time: 30 minutes

Servings: 6

Ingredients

Coconut flour – 3 Tbsp. Pumpkin pie spice – 1 tsp. Baking powder – ¼ tsp.

Baking soda – ¼ tsp. Pinch salt Pumpkin puree – ¾ cup

Swerve brown – 1/3 cup Heavy whipping cream – ¼ cup

Egg – 1 Vanilla – ½ tsp.

Directions:

Line 6 muffin cups with parchment paper and preheat the oven to 350° F.

In a bowl, whisk together the salt, baking soda, baking powder, pumpkin pie spice, and coconut flour.

In another bowl, whisk egg, vanilla, cream, sweetener, and pumpkin puree until mixed. Whisk in dry ingredients.

Pour into the muffin cups and bake until just puffed and almost set, about 25 to 30 minutes.

Remove and cool.

Refrigerate for about 1 hour.

Top with whipped cream and serve.

Nutrition:

Calories: 70

Fat: 4.1g

Carb: 5.1g

Protein: 1.7g

Sodium 120 mg

94. Brownies

Preparation time: 15 minutes

Cooking time: 20 minutes

Servings: 16

Ingredients   Butter – ½ cup, melted   Swerve sweetener – 2/3 cup   Eggs – 3

Vanilla extract – ½ tsp.   Almond flour – ½ cup   Cocoa powder – 1/3 cup

Gelatin – 1 Tbsp.   Baking powder – ½ tsp.

Salt – ¼ tsp.

Water – ¼ cup

Sugar-free chocolate chips – 1/3 cup

Directions

Grease a (8 x 8-inch) baking pan and preheat the oven to 350° F.

In a bowl, whisk together eggs, vanilla extract, sweetener, and butter.

Add the salt, baking powder, gelatin, cocoa powder, and flour and whisk until combined. Stir in the chocolate chips.

Fill the prepared baking pan with the batter.

Bake until center still a bit wet, but the edges are set, about 15 to 20 minutes.

Remove, cool, slice, and serve.

Nutrition:

Calories: 110

Fat: 9.5g

Carb: 3.6g

Protein: 3.1g

Sodium: 89 mg

95. Ice Cream

Preparation time: 15 minutes

Cooking time: 30 minutes

Servings: 8

Ingredients

Heavy whipping cream – 2 ½ cups, divided

Swerve brown – ¼ cup

Sugar substitute – ¼ cup

Butter – 2 Tbsp.

Maple extract – 1 ½ tsp.

Xanthan gum – ¼ tsp.

Chopped walnuts – 1/3 cup

Directions

In a saucepan, bring two sweeteners, and 1 ¼ cups of the whipping cream to a simmer. Lower heat and gently simmer for 30 minutes.

Remove from the heat and whisk in maple extract, and butter. Add the xanthan gum and whisk to mix well. Cool, then place in the refrigerator for about 2 hours.

Beat the remaining whipping cream in a bowl until stiff peaks. Foil in chilled cream/maple until well combined. Stir in chopped walnuts.

Freeze until firm.

Serve.

Nutrition:

Calories: 318

Fat: 31.7g

Carb: 2.9g

Protein: 2.8g

Sodium: 31 mg

96. Cheesecake Keto Fat Bombs

Preparation time: 10 Minutes

Cooking time: 10 Minutes

Servings: 12

Ingredients

5 oz. cream cheese

2 oz. frozen strawberries

2 oz. butter

2 tbsp stevia sweetener

1 tsp vanilla extract

Directions

Puree the strawberries using a blender.

In a bowl mix sweetener, vanilla, pureed strawberries and mix well.

Microwave cream cheese and combine with the rest of ingredients.

Add butter to the mixture and mix with an electric mixer.

Divide into 10-12 round silicone molds and freeze for 1-2 hours before serving.

Nutrition:

Calories: 78

Protein: 0.9g

Fat: 8 g

Carbohydrates: 0.8 g

Sodium: 62 mg

97. Keto Egg Crepes

Preparation time: 10 Minutes

Cooking time: 10 Minutes

Servings: 2

Ingredients

5 eggs

5 oz. cream cheese

1 tsp cinnamon

1 tablespoon sugar substitute

Butter

Filling

7 tablespoons butter

½ cup sugar substitute

1 tablespoon cinnamon

Directions

Blend all of the crepe ingredients until smooth.

Pour butter into the pan and cook 1-2 minutes per side.

Remove and pour mixture over the crepes.

For crepes mixture mix cinnamon and sweetener in a bowl.

Serve when ready.

Nutrition:

Calories: 918 kcal

Protein: 28.08 g

Fat: 84.75 g

Carbohydrates: 13.23 g

Sodium: 885 mg

98. Keto Naan

Preparation time: 10 Minutes

Cooking time: 30 Minutes

Servings: 4

Ingredients

½ cup coconut flour

1 tablespoon psyllium husk

1 tablespoon ghee

½ tsp baking powder

½ tsp salt

1 cup boiling water

Directions

In a bowl mix all ingredients and refrigerate.

Divine the dough into 6 balls.

Heat a cast iron skillet over medium heat and place the naan balls.

Cook for 2-3 minutes remove and serve.

Nutrition:

Calories: 6 kcal

Protein: 0.22 g

Fat: 0.06 g

Carbohydrates: 1.41 g

Sodium: 324 mg

99. Peanut Butter Cookies

Preparation time: 10 Minutes

Cooking time: 30 Minutes

Servings: 12

Ingredients

1 cup peanut butter

1 tsp vanilla

1 tsp baking powder

½ tsp salt

½ cup Keto sweetener

1 egg

Directions

Preheat oven to 325° F.

Cream together all ingredients.

Refrigerate for 15-20 minutes.

Roll dough into balls and place on a parchment paper.

Bake for 12-15 minutes.

Serve.

Nutrition:

Calories: 102 kcal

Protein: 2.27 g

Fat: 4.69 g

Carbohydrates: 12.41 g

Sodium: 427 mg

100. Buttery Keto Crepes

Preparation time: 10 Minutes

Cooking time: 10 Minutes

Servings: 2

Ingredients

3 eggs

½ tsp vanilla extract

½ tsp cinnamon

3 oz. cream cheese

2 tsp sweetener

2 tablespoons butter

Directions

In a blender place all the ingredients and blend until smooth.

In a skillet pour batter and cook each crepe for 1-2 minutes per side or until ready.

Remove and serve with berries, maple syrup or jam.

Nutrition:

Calories: 448 kcal

Protein: 16.63 g

Fat: 38.19 g

Carbohydrates: 8.95 g

Sodium: 431 mg

Chapter 24: Sauces and Dressings Recipes

101. Tzatziki

Preparation time: 10 mins

Cooking time: 0 mins

Servings: 8

Ingredients:

½ c shredded cucumber, drained

1 tsp salt 1 T olive oil 1 T fresh mint, finely chopped

2 garlic cloves

1 c full-fat Greek yogurt

1 t lemon juice

Directions:

Place shredded cucumber on a strainer for an hour or squeeze out moisture through a cheesecloth.

Mix all ingredients in a medium bowl and refrigerate.

Use as a vegetable dip, a dip for dehydrated vegetables, or a sauce for lamb, beef, or chicken. It is also a perfect accompaniment for fried summer squash.

Nutrition:

Calories: 79

Carbohydrates: 3g

Protein: 1g Fat: 7g

Sodium: 302 mg

102. Satay Sauce

Preparation time: 20 mins

Cooking time: 15 mins

Servings: 4

Ingredients:

1 can (14 oz) coconut cream (if you can't find coconut cream, coconut milk works well)

1 dry red pepper, seeds removed, chopped fine

1 clove garlic, minced

¼ c gluten-free soy sauce

1/3 c natural unsweetened peanut butter

Salt and pepper

Directions:

Place all Ingredients in a small saucepan.

Bring the mixture to a boil.

Stir while heating to mix peanut butter with other Ingredients as it melts.

After the mixture boils, turn down the heat to simmer on low heat for 5 to 10 minutes.

Remove from heat when the sauce is at the desired consistency.

Adjust seasoning to taste.

This is a good sauce for chicken or turkey. Just add the sauce during the last minutes of baking or grilling. It can also be used as a dipping sauce.

Nutrition:

Calories: 312

Carbohydrates: 7g

Protein: 7g

Fat: 30g

Sodium: 1023 mg

103. Thousand Island Salad Dressing

Preparation time: 10 mins

Cooking time: 5 mins

Servings: 8

Ingredients:

2 T olive oil

¼ c frozen spinach, thawed

2 T dried parsley

1 T dried dill

1 t onion powder

½ t salt

¼ t black pepper

1 c full-fat mayonnaise

¼ c full-fat sour cream

2 t lemon juice

Directions:

Mix all ingredients in a small bowl and enjoy!

This dressing can be covered and stored for up to 5 days.

Nutrition:

Calories: 312

Carbohydrates: 2g

Protein: 1g

Fat: 34g

Sodium: 161 mg

104. Hollandaise Sauce

Preparation time: 30 mins

Cooking time: 25 mins

Servings: 4

Ingredients:

4 egg yolks

2 T lemon juice

1 ½ sticks of butter, melted

Salt and pepper

Directions:

Heat water to boil in a saucepan.

Separate the eggs. Save the whites for another use.

Place the yolks in a heat-resistant bowl, either glass or stainless steel.

Carefully melt the butter in a saucepan without burning.

Place the bowl with the egg yolks over the simmering water to gently heat the eggs. Make sure the water is not touching the bottom of the bowl. The eggs need to be steamed, not cooked.

Add lemon juice to egg yolks.

Slowly stream the melted butter into the egg yolks while whisking. Start with a few drops of butter and then add a slow stream. Whisk the eggs the entire time until all the butter is added, and the sauce has thickened.

Season to taste with lemon juice, salt, and pepper. You can also add a dash of tabasco sauce.

Serve over poached eggs or cooked vegetables.

Nutrition:

Calories: 566

Carbohydrates: 1g

Protein: 3g

Fat: 62g

Sodium: 52 mg

105. Low Carb Strawberry Jam

Preparation time: 25 minutes

Cooking time: 20 minutes

Servings: 2

Ingredients:

Knox gelatin powder, three-fourths teaspoon

Lemon juice, one tablespoon

Water, one quarter cup

Sugar replacement, one quarter cup

Strawberries, diced, one cup

Directions:

Sprinkle the lemon juice with the gelatin and allow it to sit and thicken. Add the water, strawberries, and sugar replacement to a small pot and set it over medium heat. As soon as this mixture begins to simmer, lower the heat and let it simmer for 20 minutes. Chop up the gelatin lemon juice mix, mix it in with the warm strawberries and let it dissolve. Let the jam cool after removing the pan from the heat, then spoon the mix into a clean glass jar. This jam will remain good in the refrigerator for two weeks.

This can be made with any low carb fruit.

Nutrition:

Calories 57

Net carbs .85 grams

Fat 0 grams

Protein .66 grams

Sodium 14 mg

106. Plain Mayonnaise

Preparation time: 10 minutes

Cooking time: 0 minutes

Servings: 1

Ingredients:

Lemon juice, two teaspoons

Olive oil, one cup

Dijon mustard, one tablespoon at room temperature

Egg yolk, one at room temperature

Directions:

Cream together the mustard and the egg yolk and then pour in the oil slowly while stirring to mix. Add in the lemon juice and mix one last time and then let the mixture sit until it is thick. This will stay fresh for about four days in the refrigerator.

Nutrition:

Calories 511

Net carbs 0 grams

Fat 57 grams

Protein 1 gram

Sodium 185 mg

107. Ranch Dip

Preparation time: 1 hour

Cooking time: 0 minutes

Servings: 1

Ingredients:

Ranch seasoning, two tablespoons

Sour cream, one half cup

Mayonnaise, one cup

Directions

Mix all of the ingredients together and allow to chill for at least one hour before serving.

Nutrition:

Calories 241

Net carbs 1-gram

Fat 26 grams

Protein 1 gram

Sodium 2570 mg

108. Avocado Sauce

Preparation time: 10 minutes

Cooking time: 0 minutes

Servings: 1

Ingredients:

Pistachio nuts, two ounces

Salt, one teaspoon

Lime juice, one quarter cup

Garlic, minced, two tablespoons

Water, one quarter cup

Olive oil, two-thirds cup

Avocado, one

Parsley or cilantro, fresh, one cup

Directions:

Use a food processor or a blender to mix all of the ingredients together until they are smooth except the pistachio nuts and olive oil.

Add these at the end and mix well. If the mix is a bit thick add in a bit more oil or water. This sauce will stay fresh in the refrigerator for up to four days.

Nutrition:

Calories 490

Net carbs 5 grams

Fat 50 grams

Protein 5 grams

Sodium 2388 mg

109. Blue Cheese Dressing

Preparation time: 1 hour

Cooking time: 0 minutes

Servings: 1

Ingredients:

Parsley, fresh, two tablespoons

Black pepper, one teaspoon

Salt, one teaspoon

Heavy whipping cream, one half cup

Mayonnaise, one half cup

Greek yogurt, three-fourths cup

Blue cheese, five ounces

Directions:

Break the blue cheese up into small chunks in a large bowl. Stir in the heavy cream, mayonnaise, and yogurt. Mix in the parsley, salt, and pepper and let the dressing sit for one hour, so the flavors mix well. This dressing will be good in the refrigerator for three days.

Nutrition:

Calories 477

Net carbs 4 grams

Fat 47 grams

Protein 10 grams

Sodium 3279 mg

110. Salsa Dressing

Preparation time: 1 hour

Cooking time: 0 minutes

Servings: 1

Ingredients:

Garlic, minced, one tablespoon

Chili powder, one teaspoon

Apple cider vinegar, three tablespoons

Mayonnaise, two tablespoons

Sour cream, two tablespoons

Olive oil, one quarter cup

Salsa, one half cup

Directions

Add all of the ingredients to a large bowl and mix well. Pour into a glass jar and let the dressing chill in the refrigerator for at least one hour.

This dressing will stay good in the refrigerator for three days.

Nutrition:

Calories 200

Net carbs 2 grams

Fat 21 grams

Protein 1-gram

Sodium 1126 mg

Conclusion

Congratulations for making it this far! By now, I trust you already have a good understanding of the Ketogenic Diet and how it applies to you as you enjoy your 50s. Obviously, our goal here is to provide a Keto Diet guideline that works for you, taking into account your unique situation so that the best and most effective results can be enjoyed.

The most important thing I want you to learn from this book is this: it's *never* too late to make that change! It's never too late to try something new for self-improvement! Don't get set in your ways, especially if your old ways don't do much for your overall health. I want you to know that you have what it takes to be better not just physically, but also mentally and psychologically. Of course, the mere fact that you purchased and read this book is a good start. I know you can do it – all you have to do is take that first important step.

So, what should you do next? I want you to go to the kitchen and take a long, good look at the refrigerator. I want you to start evaluating its contents and make a distinction between what's good for you, and what's not based on the Ketogenic Diet we just discussed. I want you to take that important first step of deciding on a Keto-friendly breakfast, lunch, and dinner for tomorrow. Choose from any of the recipes mentioned above or choose any method you deem best!

Printed in Great Britain
by Amazon